WHO NEEDS A HORSE THAT FLIES?

Who Needs a Horse That Flies?

Essays on Poetry and Pretense

by

Samuel Hazo

Pittsburgh:
Serif Press
2024

Thanks to the *Pittsburgh Quarterly*, *Renascence* and the *Pittsburgh Post-Gazette* for permission to reprint, as well as to the University of Notre Dame Press for "Provence of the Six Winds" from *The Stroke of a Pen* (2011). Gratitude is also due to the Richard Wilbur estate for all quotes from his poems in "One Definite Mozart."

Contents

To Jake and Cristina Grefenstette

and

Christopher Bailey

Who Needs a Horse That Flies?

Most of what we do or make, for good or ill, originates in the imagination. This makes it the most indispensable and powerful of all our human potentialities. I am not speaking here only of art or those word-creations that we call poems. I am speaking of anything that we first dream or, if you will, conceive and then realize as facts—facts that have the imagination as their source. This can be anything from how we are dressed this minute (which we imaginatively planned before we chose the clothes we chose) to the building or house in which we now find ourselves (which originated in the imagination of the architect who designed it) to the city and the society in which we live (the former originating in the imagination of the original pioneers and planners, and the latter originating in the imagination of Thomas Jefferson and the unique group of deist politicians known as the Founding Fathers). In that sense we can regard the entire experience with American democracy for more than two centuries as the participation of citizens in an ongoing imaginative experiment. In other words, it was imagined that people could live communally no longer on the basis of tribal loyalty or race or heredity but on allegiance to a citizen-created constitution—a government of, by and for the people in the words of Lincoln's great "poem" subsequently called "The Gettysburg Address." Lewis H. Lapham, the former editor of *Harper's* and a superb essayist in his own right, confirmed this when he wrote that democracy "is a shared work of the imagination." And we can logically conclude that any breakdown in democracy can be attributed to a breakdown in the imagination, which permits the former allegiances to race, blood or custom to re-assert themselves. Thornton Wilder has even gone so far as to claim that violence itself can be attributed to a failure of imagination.

Thought of in this way, the imagination, which Samuel Taylor Coleridge called an "esemplastic power," is the father of both invention and, where literature and art are concerned, creation. Let us consider architecture as an example of the imagination at work since architecture involves both creation and invention. Architecture, which has been defined as the "creation of artificial space," permitted man to live in other than natural shelters like caves because at some point a human being imagined that it could be otherwise. Stone, wood, thatch and even ice were used to create dwellings of various types, but it was the inchoate architectural imagination that conceived of them as habitable and protective. And, adjusting to man's nature and his social demands, architecture slowly evolved beyond housing into everything from palaces to prisons. Of course, such an evolution, as in all things creative or inventive, is subject to other influences, not all of them beneficent. A man who owned a city block, for example, could derive income from stores, offices or places of business built at street level. But in the name of entrepreneurism (the contemporary password for any profit-making enterprise, which in turn is probably prompted by something as undisguised as greed) that same landowner could imagine additional income if he built a second, third or fourth floor on top of the street level real estate. And continuing upward to higher floors he could add to his income as long as the ascent was architecturally possible. Thus, the skyscraper, despite the PR ballyhoo, is nothing but a way of acquiring more and more income from more and more stories. It is all answerable to the creative impulse as influenced by a desire for more and more profit. That and the invention of the elevator, with further refinements added by Mr. Otis and his elevator company, show that the creative impulse, however admirable and "esemplastic," can be wrested to other purposes. It's certainly not confined to architecture. When the imagination is diseased by ideology or spiritualism disguised as revealed religion, we often have societies that in time degenerate into fundamentalist barbarism. The concocted belief in what they imagined as their own superiority motivated the Nazis to slaughter millions in the name of purification. The current policy of the United States in the Middle East, which is dubbed "humanitarian intervention," is already being identified by historians and others as a tragedy begotten of historical naivete and hubris, and the results in deaths, physical and psychological maimings and outright waste are in the news every day to remind us of what can happen when the imagination goes awry.

If we consider speech and its representation in print as a form of creation, what challenges does this present to the imagination? And what can be said of oral or printed speech that we identify as poetry? It is universally conceded that speech in whatever language is what differentiates man from the other animals. But speech has many levels. There is the level of conversation, petition or gossip, the level of simple or complex communication, the level of rhetoric and so on. All of these serve a purpose, to be sure, but they all lack what poetry by its very nature possesses —the capacity to engage those who experience it at several levels at once, i.e., the literal level (what the words actually mean), the suggestive level (what the words sound like or how their meanings may be enhanced when placed next to other words), the symbolic level (what it evokes over and above its literal, tonal and associative meanings). Straight communication is rarely concerned with the last two considerations, but poets are. When they are able to bring multiple capacities of language into play, they somehow create in those who read or hear them more than straight communication. It is a sense of communion—co-union. We irresistibly become one with the subject. When Mercutio, for example, is asked if he had been wounded after his skirmish with Tybalt in *Romeo and Juliet*, he could simply have said yes. If he were a medical student, he could have said, "It's a single stab wound three inches to the right of the navel and just below the lowest rib." Instead, realizing that he has been mortally wounded, he says with his usual flair, "'Tis not deep as a well nor wide as a church door, but it will do." Which of those three responses has the more poetic dimension?

The vision that is given by what words mean, what they suggest, what they evoke by their tones or half-tones and by their rhythm is language expressed in full. In this context it is relevant to remember that the Greeks conceived of poetry as a winged horse named Pegasus. Something about the way a horse cantered or galloped approximated for the Greeks the rhythms of poetic language and the way those rhythms can come to engage our total attention when we hear them. But in addition to hooves, Pegasus has wings. This suggests to me that the Greeks were not only sensitive to poetic rhythm but to the visionary power of words to ascend or, in keeping with the metaphor, to transcend the moment, to fly.

We live in a society of transmissions, explicitly stated concepts, sloganeering, bites of sound (words tailored to the time allowed to say them), the siren songs of slang and advertising. In other words, we are inundated by everything from straight talk to finessed lying. Language in this sense does not and cannot create moments of intimacy or union. Poetry somehow does, and this is as primal and universal and "feelingly" understandable as a scream, a moan, a cry of unbearable pleasure or pain. It stops us. It transcends the moment. And above all, it expresses who we are in words that are unmistakably human. If we place that next to the demagoguery and all the various flavors of lying from political correctness to the syrupy deceptions of diplomacy and the malicious falsehoods we call slander, we realize that without the candor of felt speech we are left only with inferiorities—a Babel of "sound and fury signifying nothing." This is why poetry is not an optional but an essential and ongoing engagement. "The survival of poetry, in fact the survival of humans and their words," warns Wendell Berry, "depends upon the cultivation of better language." And he continues: "Poems worthy of the name, and of the effort to make them, are made of necessity by inspiration and because they are needed."

Talking about poetry's qualities and capabilities is never as good as letting poems speak for themselves. I have chosen a few examples, beginning with one of the most recognizable and going on from there.

We have all heard the truism that appearances can be deceptive. We may or may not accept that as true, but we can understand and accept it simply as an idea. We may nod yes or no, but such a response does not engage us totally. In a similar and more particular way we have heard that money is a solution to many, if not all, problems. In fact, so many think of money as a total solution that the "have-nots" come to envy the "haves" because they think that the "haves" have it all, have everything. When one of the "haves" does something not in keeping with our expectation of how "haves" should behave, we are often stunned. We say, "Why did he or she do that?" The unsaid implication is that the person asking the question would not, if he or she were in a position of a "have," do such a thing. These are quite common attitudes—the deception created by appearances and the assumption, especially in our society, that wealth is the ultimate desideratum and the ultimate answer. In a much-anthologized and well-known poem entitled "Richard Cory," Edwin Arlington Robinson presents us with an ironic vision of a deeper reality behind what I have just summarized.

Whenever Richard Cory went down town,
We people on the pavement looked at him:
He was a gentleman from sole to crown,
Clean-favored, and imperially slim.

And he was always quietly arrayed,
And he was always human when he talked;

But still he fluttered pulses when he said,
"Good-morning," and he glittered when he walked.

And he was rich,—yes, richer than a king,—
And admirably schooled in every grace:
In fine, we thought that he was everything
To make us wish that we were in his place.

So on we worked, and waited for the light,
And went without the meat, and cursed the bread;
And Richard Cory, one calm summer night,
Went home and put a bullet through his head.

The poem, i.e., the effect of this poem on us, will not let us retreat into abstraction or platitudes. All that I said in preface to the actual poem simply does not have the visceral effect that the poem has. The poem *is* what it describes. It presents, in the terse language of William Carlos Williams, the thing itself and not the idea of the thing. "No ideas but in things," insisted Williams, which is another way of saying that the thing and the poem must be one and the same.

This is only as it should be. Ideas simply remain ideas unless and until they are embodied. The aforementioned poet and critic, Wendell Berry, not only supports Williams' insistence but finds support in connection with the Incarnation—"And the Word was made flesh, and dwelt among us." As long as "the Word made flesh" was only an idea, it remained an abstraction. But once embodied in the person of Jesus Christ it was unignorable. And the results speak and have spoken for themselves for centuries in the best and worst of ways.

It is in the world of the incarnate word that we find our true selves, and it is the imagination that takes us there. It is not what we see but what we imagine we see, hear what we imagine we hear and so on through all the senses that we truly experience the world. It is probably what William Blake was emphatic about when he wrote: "We are led to believe a lie/When we see not through but with the eye." Seeing through the eye is what gives us a true vision of what is there—the face behind the mask, the reality behind the appearance, the mystery that suddenly illuminates the ordinary and for a moment transforms it into something that is unforgettable.

Some years ago, I had a student who was also a registered nurse with supervisory responsibilities. Older and more mature than the others, she wrote the following single line when I asked the class to write what it feels like to be hopelessly disappointed. The nurse prefaced her response by saying that she found it impossible stop feeling love for a man who no longer loved her. She wrote: "Love for me is like the bubble inside the glass stem of a wineglass—a defect." Such a description is not only succinct but proves without any need for substantiation that less is more, poetically speaking. Likewise, I have always treasured Norman Mailer's damning description of Georgia Governor Lester Maddox during the Civil Rights campaign in the South. Maddox distributed axe handles free of charge to recalcitrant white voters in Georgia so that they could use them to club black voters when they came to the voting booths—a practice he defended gleefully in his public appearances. Mailer in a single sentence captured the look and character of the man: "Governor Maddox has the face of a mean baby with glasses on it."

In a different but related genre the same succinctness and pith can be found in what is called proverbial literature. Such proverbs incline to poetry because they are often saying something much more profound than what they are literally saying, as in: "Peace makes money, and money makes war." "I went into the shroud business; nobody died." "A donkey appears to me like a horse translated into Dutch." "A peaceful mouse learned that kindness is wasted on the vicious."

Short takes like these are not what we think of when we think of poetry, but they are poetic and memorable in nature because they spring from the imagination, from the visionary character of our sensibility. And that holds true even when we find it in what is customarily called prose. Here is a passage from a book of essays called *Mortal Lessons* by Richard Selzer, a professor and surgeon emeritus at Yale:

> I stand by the bed where a young woman lies, her face postoperative, her mouth twisted in palsy, clownish. A tiny twig of the facial nerve, the one to the muscles of her mouth, has been severed. She will be thus from now on. The surgeon had followed with religious fervor the curve of her flesh.
>
> Her young husband is in the room. He stands on the opposite side of the bed, and together they seem to dwell in evening lamplight, isolated from me, private. Who are they, I ask myself, he and this wry mouth I have made, who gaze at and touch each other so generously, greedily? The young woman speaks.
>
> "Will my mouth always be like this?" she asks.
>
> "Yes," I say, "it will. It is because the nerve was cut."
>
> She nods, and is silent. The young man smiles.
>
> "I like it," he says. "It is kind of cute."
>
> All at once I know who he is. I understand, and I lower my gaze. One is not bold in an encounter with a god. Unmindful, he bends to kiss her crooked mouth, and I so close I can see how he twists his own lips to accommodate to hers, to show her that their kiss still works. I remember that the gods appeared in ancient Greece as mortals, and I hold my breath and let the wonder in...

It is how Selzer poetically evokes the beauty of this moment that makes it heartbreakingly true and unforgettable. We cannot forget it even if we try.

I have chosen these examples to show that even in the most common day-to-day occurrences—a scene on a city street and a brief episode in a hospital—poetry can be seen and summoned by the words of a visionary writer. Perhaps that is why May Swenson, herself an excellent poet, was prompted to write in a now long since filed essay in the late *Saturday Review* that the poet was possibly the last generalist in a society like ours that may be placing too high a value on specialization. The usual specialist tends to see reality through the prison of his own specialty, and more often than not that is as far as he looks. The generalist is interested in everything. The poet is such a generalist, not in the sense of acknowledging that everything is of equal importance but affirming this importance by focusing on some small detail that reveals the essence of the moment to the rest of us.

If we review these various assumptions, definitions and examples, it is possible to come up with some crucial insights. One is that we, unlike all other creatures, are able to imagine more than the obvious by seeing "through the eye." This empowers us to distinguish the false from the true and to say so in such terms that others can feel what we are saying. Take the following short poem by the great contemporary German poet Hans Magnus Enzensberger called "Portrait of a House Detective." In this translation by Michael Hamburger we have what seems like an unremarkable portrait of a somewhat eccentric and sloppy loner. He has built-in prejudices and peeves and hatreds, and he comes across as one of those people one would be inclined to ignore. But by the time we finish the poem, we see that this loner was in retrospect not at all ignorable. His very peevishness eventually was secondary to his ultimate work in life, and the entire world paid for it.

> he lolls in the supermarket
> under the plastic sun,
> the white patches on his face
> are rage, not consumption,

a hundred packets of crispy crackers
(*because they are so nourishing*)
he sets ablaze with his eyes,
a piece of margarine
(the same brand as mine:
goldlux, because it's so delicious)
he picks up with his moist hand
and squeezes it till it drips.

he's twenty-nine,
idealistic,
sleeps badly and alone
with pamphlets and blackheads,
hates the boss and the supermarket,
communists, women,
landlords, himself
and his bitten fingernails
full of margarine (*because
it's so delicious),* under
his arty hairstyle mutters
to himself like a pensioner.
that one
will never get anywhere.
wittler, i think, he's called,
wittler, hittler, or something like that.

The absence of poetry from our daily discourse and our public life leaves a total vacuum because there is no substitute for it. Pretending that it is not essential or ignoring it entirely when it does appear is similar to situations when individuals or entire peoples choose to ignore weather reports. True, weather reports are not always correct, but even in their fallibility they are without alternative in prognosticating weather. Dismissing or trivializing them can be seen as foolish or even fatal by those who have ignored tornado and tsunami warnings. In a certain sense, poems are like spiritual weather reports, and we ignore them to our peril.

In 1963 President John Kennedy addressed this very subject in a speech at Amherst: "When power leads man towards arrogance, poetry reminds him of his limitations. When power narrows the areas of man's concern, poetry reminds him of the richness and diversity of his existence. When power corrupts, poetry cleanses. For art establishes the basic human truth which must serve as the touchstone of our judgment. The artist, however faithful to his personal vision of reality, becomes the last champion of the individual mind and sensibility against an intrusive society and an officious state. The great artist is thus a solitary figure.... In pursuing his perception of reality, he must often sail against the current of his times. This is not a popular role."

If these words are true as far as they go, why isn't poetry a central presence in our public life? If poetry is human utterance in its most perfect form—felt thought feelingly expressed—why is it marginalized or overlooked entirely in public speech? The answers to both questions vary in their wrongness.

Some say that poetry is acceptable as long as it is "pleasant," which is like saying that poetry should have the same relationship that Muzak has to music—tolerable as long as it stays soothingly in the background. Others say that poetry should remain at the Hallmark level—the detritus of emotional cliché. Still others point to weddings, funerals and certain honorific events and claim that poetry is often given a place in such proceedings. And this is true. But what passes for poetry then has usually been "written for the occasion." Having heard many of these, I felt that they had been willed (and not inspired) into existence, proving repeatedly that true poems are rarely if ever created on demand.

To cite similar examples in the public domain, consider those times when poets were invited to recite at the presidential inaugurations of

Kennedy, Carter, Clinton and Obama—Robert Frost, James Dickey, Maya Angelou, Miller Williams and Elizabeth Alexander. It was fortunate in retrospect that Frost was unable to read the versified treatise he had written for Kennedy's inauguration because the January sun prevented him from seeing the text. Instead (and quite appropriately) he spoke from memory a previously written and infinitely better poem called "The Gift Outright." Dickey and Williams, who are genuine poets by any standard, recited sincerely felt lines that were not in any way comparable to their best work. Maya Angelou simply rhapsodized, and what Elizabeth Alexander recited is best left without comment.

Leaving inaugurations aside, why is it that audiences for "poetry hearings" are spare when compared to those for plays, operas, stand-up comedians or the elaborate noise of rock concerts? Is it because we are a prose-and-screen oriented people who are so inundated daily with advertising copy, journalism, the propaganda of political jargon and gossip that we have no eye or ear for poetry? Is it because noise has hidden poetic values that some of us are missing? Is it simply due to the fact that many poets who read well on the page do not recite well on the stage? Or is it because we have weak attention spans that are not up to what poetry demands? Is this the case in countries other than our own? Decades ago I was just completing a State Department-sponsored lecture tour to Lebanon, Jordan, Egypt and Greece. In Greece, I met the Nobel poet George Seferis (Georgios Seferiadis) before his appearance in the Greek Hellenic Union in Athens. Having served the government for much of his life out of Greece, Seferis faced a packed auditorium of people primed to hear their national poet for the first time in his own country. Loudspeakers were set up so that hundreds of people outside the Union could hear him, and thousands heard him in simultaneous broadcast throughout Greece. Such events do not happen in the United States.

But in Greece, the Arab countries and throughout Europe there is a built-in respect for poetic tradition, and this has consequences. Greece is a nation of eleven and half million people, but it has had only two Nobel awardees, Seferis and Odysseus Elytis. Ireland, a country of four and a half million, has had three: William Butler Yeats, Samuel Beckett and Seamus Heaney. The United States with a population of three hundred million has had five—T. S. Eliot, Joseph Brodsky, Czeslaw Milosz, Bob Dylan and Louise Gluck. Eliot was born in St. Louis but became an Anglicized American. Brodsky and Milosz wrote in their native languages, and I still have my doubts about Dylan and Gluck. Who wrote in an American idiom? And why were such poets as Archibald MacLeish, Robert Frost, Marianne Moore, Richard Wilbur, Robert Lowell, William Stafford and Randall Jarrell overlooked?

Perhaps Americans are indifferent to their poets because poets are genuine seers; they write and say what exists beneath appearances without verbiage or deceit. Like the Hebrew prophets they do not write to please. I am speaking here of poets in fact and not in name, not versifiers, tiddly-rhymers, networkers or charlatans. Americans who are susceptible to military vanity, particularly in our misguided wars from the fifties to the present moment, might modify their attitude after considering one of the consequences of war as described in the final line of Randall Jarrell's "The Death of the Ball Turret Gunner"—"When I died, they washed me out of the turret with a hose." For those who want a glimpse of the commercial core of American civic life, I would offer Robert Lowell's conclusion to "For the Union Dead" with its terse description of traffic in downtown Boston: "A savage servility/slides by on grease." And then there is Louis Simpson's "To the Western World" whose final lines read like an epitaph: "The generations labor to possess/and grave by grave we civilize the ground."

And what about William Stafford's inserted couplet in "Religion Back Home" that makes us smile before we see all wars from Troy to our present tragic and illegal adventurism in Stafford's semi-playful words: "Our Father Who Art in Heaven/Can lick their Father Who Art in Heaven." And finally, there is an indicting couplet by e. e. cummings that is not without merit: "A politician is an arse upon/which everyone has sat except a man."

These are only a handful of examples I have selected to demonstrate the constant relevance of poetry to public life and public speech. The books from which they are drawn are out there and available. And there are thousands of others throughout the world from time of the Sumerians to right now. If we refuse to read and share them, who can deny that we will be the poorer for it?

Is Peace Possible?

In February 2022 Russian forces were ordered by Putin to engage in nuclear war exercises. This was obviously the result of reactions of the United States and its NATO partners to Russia's unprovoked invasion of Ukraine. Later Putin said that there would be what he called unprecedented consequences if resistance to the Ukrainian invasion continued. This was understood to be a veiled threat but did not weaken the resistance to the invasion by those countries that opposed it. Putin had made threats of this kind before in 2008. Because Russia was and remains a nuclear power, such threats, though perceived at the time to be a ploy or a bluff, could not be permanently dismissed as diplomacy by another name. Knowing the character of Putin, no one could say that the reality of nuclear war was beyond possibility.

Even though sane people realize that nuclear war on a limited or total scale would ravage the planet, they also would have to admit that war could be initiated by faulty judgment or a character flaw in one with the power to initiate such a war. Putin seems to have the kind of character that does not rule out such a possibility.

My research into the possibility of nuclear war, should it happen, begins with identifying those countries that qualify as nuclear powers. The main possible combatants, of course, are the United States and Russia, although other nuclear powers have come into being and could become involved. If war would be initiated by the most dominant powers, it is estimated that on the first day of conflict 34.1 million human beings would be killed and 57.1 million wounded. The United States and Russia alone, having more than 3000 nuclear bombs apiece aimed at specific targets in each country, would be the chief destroyers. For Russia the targeted cities would be Washington, New York and military sites. For the United States the targets would be Moscow and seven other cities or military sites. I leave to your imaginations what the breadth of the destruction would be if other nuclear powers were involved.

If the war continued beyond the first day, it is estimated that there would be more than 400 to 500 million dead and wounded. There would subsequently be roughly 348 million casualties related to fallout or temperature change. In time there would also be some 772 million deaths or disabilities caused by poisonous soot in the atmosphere.

All of these possible lethal or crippling results from nuclear attacks could be blamed on any of the following nuclear powers: United States, Russia, China, France, India, Israel, North Korea, Pakistan and the United Kingdom. Enmities exist between some of these nations, but so far they have not risen to the level of motivating any one to attack the other. Assuming that only the fear of devastating annihilation has deterred such attacks through the last half of the twentieth and the first decades of the twenty-first century, it is possible to conclude that such fear is a force for nuclear peace if only in the most atavistic sense. It certainly does not have the nobility of Kant's hope for "perpetual peace" nor any of the sentiments expressed in Pope John XXIII's *Pacem in Terris*. What we derive from the silent weapon of deterrence is but a logical defensive reaction to Hagel's concept of man as a predator in disguise who must be contained, opposed, subdued.

As far as the United States is concerned, a policy of deterrence has certainly not turned us away from "smaller" or "chosen" wars, any one of which could have had or could still have nuclear consequences. As I have mentioned in a related essay, every administration since 1950 has in varying ways and for different reasons involved us in a war of choice. The only one that was presented to Congress for its approval and support was the Persian Gulf War. This was requested by the elder Bush to permit American and allied forces to drive Saddam Hussein out of Kuwait. Constitutionally speaking, Congress alone has the power to commit the United States to war, but all the wars since 1950, except the Persian Gulf War, were given names like "police actions" and the like to absolve Congress of its responsibility.

The wars in which we were involved in Korea, Lebanon (twice), Vietnam, Grenada, Iran-Contra, Afghanistan and Iraq were chosen and "declared" by the President. The cost in dollars was in the trillions. The cost to date in the lives of American men and women is in excess of 85,000. As for the number of Americans wounded in these chosen wars, the number in Vietnam alone is more than 8 times the 58,000 killed there. Veteran suicides fluctuate between 20 and 22 each day on the average, and that figure has been steady from 2000 to the present, which translates into more than 7,000 a year. From all our chosen wars, the number of Koreans, Vietnamese, Afghans and Iraqis killed is astronomical. The number of North Vietnamese killed is over 2,000,000 while South Vietnamese losses range around 1,000,000, including those left to the tender mercies of the Vietcong after the American departure. In Iraq, in addition to the tens of thousands of Iraqis who fled into Syria, Lebanon and Turkey, more than 500,000 were killed in Iraq, and that's a conservative figure. American casualties are in the thousands, and "no weapons of mass destruction" were ever found, as both UN Inspector Hans Blix originally and Colin Powell belatedly knew would be the case. In Lebanon the Reagan administration sent Marines to bolster the Lebanese government against a suspected Shiite insurgency. Hundreds of Marines were stationed south of Beirut in an area controlled by Shiites. As their commander later reported in a book he wrote that condemned the mission, the Marines were shelled repeatedly. One night a truck loaded with explosives was driven by a suicide bomber into a building where Marines were asleep. Hundreds were killed in the detonation—the largest single-day loss of Marine lives since Iwo Jima. Shortly thereafter, all the Marines who were left were evacuated from Lebanon—another foreign policy blunder paid for in blood.

The tragic irony of such chosen wars is that they invariably end in stalemate or worse. Technically we are still at war with North Korea. Panicked flights characterized our departure from Vietnam. Ongoing strife riddles Iraq. Policies related to them are rife with deception. The claim, for example, that the expansion of the Vietnamese War was because of the Tonkin Gulf incident (that never happened) has been discredited. Attempts to shift the blame for the war on Kennedy rather than Johnson have been debunked by McGeorge Bundy's biographer (also his chief of staff) who wrote that Kennedy wanted to withdraw troops from Vietnam but knew he could not until he was re-elected.

Chosen wars are usually limited. The ones I have mentioned have been limited, but it is never known in advance when one of them could lead to something more than local. Even if nothing widening happens, a comment by historian William L. Cohn cannot be ignored: "Endless war is the destruction of civil society." All we have to do is look at what has become of us since 2003 to see how true this is. As a society we have become more militaristic, more concerned with security, more intolerant of dissent, more top-heavy with wealth controlled by the oligarchic few and more inured to violence than we have ever been. We average 20,000 homicides per year compared with 17 in the past five years in Japan (where owning a gun or a sword is illegal), 29 per year in Norway, 93 in Greece, 549 in England, 363 in Spain and 57 in Switzerland.

What about the cost in dollars required to support troops committed abroad and the depleting effect this has on civilian needs at home? Prior to the invasion of Iraq, the Bush-Cheney-Rumsfeld-Wolfowitz-Perle cabal believed it had the right to change regimes because it had the power to do so. For moral and other reasons the American public disagreed.

Anti-war marchers numbered in the millions. And they were joined by marchers in Canada, Europe, the Near East, Asia and Australia. Historians determined this was the largest anti-war march in recorded history. Informed public sources supported the protesters. They knew that benefits of the invasion would give American corporations access to Iraqi oil (the largest oil fields in the Middle East apart from Saudi Arabia) and would dismiss Iraq as a threat to Israel. Iraq was duly invaded, and the authors of the invasion retired to their sequestered estates. With Iraq occupied, the cost of supporting American troops in the Middle East increased to a daily figure of $420,000,000, but the ultra-wealthy could care less.

Why is this desire to impose our will on another country (if the imposition is possible) so persistent in American foreign policy? It's national egotism in its most naked form, and the costs created and debts incurred are gargantuan. Iraq and Afghanistan are two of the most recent examples of this propensity, but Vietnam was the precursor of both, and the cost in lives and funding was not considered lethal enough to be a deterrent to further adventurism. The ultra-wealthy who want to privatize Social Security and eliminate Medicare as a way to restore the budget deficits caused by these wars would only make the situation worse. Robert Reich, the economist and journalist, suggests as much in his recent and clairvoyant book *The Common Good* when he writes that there is less and less concern for what is in the best interests of all. Why? One reason might be that the indebted, who constitute all but the ultra-wealthy, are too busy paying off their debts to worry about the nation's.

The late Tony Judt, who has few peers as a historian, addressed himself to this same condition in his last book *Ill Fares the Land*: "Much of what is 'natural' today dates from the 1980's obsession with wealth, the cult of privatization and the private sector, the growing disparities of rich and poor, and, above all, the rhetoric that accompanies the uncritical admiration for unfettered markets...and the delusion of endless growth."

For Tony Judt and Robert Reich the root of the problem is spiritual. As a people and as a government, we are less altruistic, more self-centered, more acquisitive and less generous. This has distracted us from facing an ultimate nuclear threat and from creating enhancements in our social life. In the 1960's, building on the New Deal's creation of Social Security and the GI Bill of Rights, there was the Kennedy-initiated and Johnson-shepherded agenda of Medicare, Medicaid, the Civil Rights Act, food stamps, Headstart, the National Endowment for the Arts, the National Endowment for the Humanities, the Peace Corps, the Student Loan Program, the Corporation for Public Broadcasting combined with Eisenhower's Interstate Highways Program and later Obama's Affordable Care Act. There has been nothing to compare with that since.

Against this historical background, what should be done and how should we think now to forestall a nuclear disaster? My first suggestion is that we should ally ourselves with the nuclear treaty that Kennedy induced Krushchev to sign in the early sixties and explore the implications for further disarmament. Secondly, we should encourage alliances between nations on the basis of a need for a common defense and, in the interim, as a way of sharing information that could lead to improvements in private and public life and even diffuse minor conflicts before they evolve into secondary wars or the ultimate war.

There is one laudable precedent for this. A singular effort was made after World War II to forestall future wars, primarily in Europe, when the Schuman Plan was initiated by Jean Monnet and Robert Schuman. The overall thrust of the plan was not a pious plea for peace on earth to men of good will but an official agreement between France and Germany that would make them economically and even militarily interdependent in ways that would make war something that would be in the worst interests of both. Schuman was even said to have taken a vow of celibacy so he could devote himself totally to finding ways that would make the plan possible for both countries. In specific terms the plan would eventually make Germany reliant on France for the coal needed for the production of steel. With steel being central to the economies of both countries, the results of such cooperation would place national interest above all else.

Other European countries were gradually attracted to form similar alliances and partnerships, and this eventually created the European Union. What is important to take from this one example is to see how much its success supported peace—peace in the most realistic and interdependent sense. This was a creative peace and not a dicey peace following successive cold wars. It was similar to the visionary courage that created the European Recovery Act or, as it is historically known, the Marshall Plan. The United States allocated the equivalent of $130,000,000,000 to help in the economic recovery of Austria, Belgium, Denmark, France, West Germany, Great Britain, Greece, Ireland, Italy, Luxembourg, the Netherlands, Norway, Sweden, Switzerland and Turkey. Peace between them has prevailed since 1945! Such alliances are no final guarantee against nuclear wars initiated by suicidal dictators. But deterrence is built into their very purpose. They show that alliances rooted in need, not greed, are not only exemplary but difficult—even for despots and dictators with nuclear ambitions—to ignore.

The Dangerous Necessity of Beauty

At one time I took for granted the traditional definition of beauty—*id quod visum placet*—that which when seen pleases. Eventually I came to see that this was much too narrow a definition. It did not include what could be called beautiful when heard, touched, tasted, felt or otherwise experienced. That is why Robert Frost's saying "Everything beautiful, that's truly beautiful, is dangerous..." disturbed me when I read it. Why dangerous? The last thing I associated with beauty was danger. The more I thought of it, the more I wondered if he meant dangerous in the sense of disruptive. The beautiful certainly has the capacity to disrupt, to stop time, however briefly, whenever it's encountered, to halt the ongoing historical flow of life simply by being itself. It transcends history and outlives, usually unforgettably, the time of its happening. At such moments we are temporarily stunned and transformed, often for the better.

Every experience we have with beauty mocks time in its passing. In this sense beauty has a great deal in common with love. When we experience the beautiful, we not only want to stay in its presence, but we want to be one with it.

The pull to unity is irresistible. If it's a sight, we try to keep the memory fresh or preserve it in a photograph. If it's a song, we want to hear it again and again until we know it as our own by singing it. The experience of beauty—like the experience of genuine love—moves inexorably toward unity. We want desperately to become totally identified with the thing that we have found beautiful. And once identified with it, we know the fear of losing it or having it fade over time. Frost's ascribing danger to beauty in this sense seems absolutely correct.

Then there is the fact of beauty's brevity. It is a platitude to say that beauty loses in intensity what it might gain in duration if it is protracted. A hibiscus, for example, offers its dish-sized blooms for only a few days, if that. And the same timetable applies to most other flowers. Similarly, physical beauty in human beings is subject to the minuses caused by aging. And life itself, if considered beautiful for the miracle it is, is quite brief in the scheme of things, no matter how long it lasts. All that lasts is the memory of how beautiful it was, and that, as we know from observing those who have suffered loss and whose memory of what was lost is painful regardless of what legacy has been left, often makes the loss even more poignant.

I do not mean to suggest that beauty's brevity is always solemn. It may be sadly joyous as a spiritual resurrection of sorts. But whether sad or joyous, such moments are at the mercy of time, and that time is always brief.

For this reason, both John Keats and Edgar Allen Poe believed that beauty and sadness were inseparable. Keats expressed this elegiacally in his "Ode on Melancholy," and Poe touched on the same theme when he wrote of the death of a beautiful woman, whether her name was Lenore or Annabel Lee. And the feeling is common with all of us. To live in full for the time given is never time enough. It is possibly the realization of this fact *a priori* that makes the very realization dangerous. Why? It could result in an individual's refusal to take the dare of life, to balk at any action at all by foreknowledge of its brevity, to live on rather than live in full.

Artists or writers who are inspired to perpetuate the temporarily but unforgettably beautiful in a work of art or in words confront the same conundrum. No matter how consummate the art or the craft, what results is a replica of the irreplaceable original—a replica of life rather than life itself.

Seeing or reading such works can leave one with an agony of regret as well as with a more humane appreciation. Thus, Keats could refer in his "Ode to a Grecian Urn" to the "cold pastoral" depicted on the urn as just that—a cold replica. Its beauty is rooted more in what it evokes than what it is. This is why the brevity of beauty may bring about in some a sense of semi-despair—a passivity that sours the experience of beauty even as it is being experienced. Instead of treasuring the moment and permitting it to deepen and have its momentary way with us, we focus only on its inevitable passing. This really immunizes us against beauty and keeps us from responding to its full effect on us.

However extolled, appreciated or vulgarized, it is true without statistics or documentation that beauty is indispensable to any life to keep it from becoming dehumanized, depraved or otherwise shriveled. More readily than men, women seem intuitively to know this and respond accordingly by beautifying themselves, their surroundings or the lives of those dearest to them. To be without beauty or love in their lives would constitute a living hell for most women. Men, though many would be reluctant to admit it, would be similarly impoverished.

As I implied earlier, the time when beauty becomes most dangerous or disruptive is at the time of its demise—when what it was in full is not what it has become. For example, I know many people who grow extremely depressed when autumn comes. For them the prime seasons are spring and summer—the months when foliage, flowers and grass are in the fullness of growth. They regard autumn as the season of slow dying before the cold and final death of winter arrives.

The changes that time imposes on the human body also instill a common dolor. Former athletes, for example, in their 50s and 60s do not have the same poise and prowess that they had in their 20s and 30s. This often leads to depression, and, in extreme cases, drunkenness or suicide.

Since beauty is more esteemed by women than by men, it's not uncommon to see women in their fifties and sixties attempt to resurrect some echo of their former beauty. Cosmetics, hair restoration and various forms of plastic surgery are seen as necessities rather than mere alternatives or options.

It is with the sight or the depiction of the female figure in its prime that the association of beauty and danger has always been most obvious to some. Fundamentalist Islamic adherents believe that all but the eyes of women should be covered in public. The depiction of the human figure, male or female, in the art of such societies is forbidden. One finds similar attitudes toward the nude figure in puritanical Christian sects, Catholic and as well as Protestant. The obvious reason goes beyond mere modesty. It seems rooted in the belief that depicting the body, particularly the female body, is catering to satisfying what moralists have called the "lust of the eyes." In certain societies such strictures do not exist, but there is an openly admitted belief that the female figure in its prime is one of the most beautiful sights in nature. Both men and women concur in this. And in art there is no scarcity of paintings of the female nude in numerous cultures. This applies to photography as well, and I am not including pornography in this statement. The crux of the matter is that observing a beautiful female nude in fact or in art usually does not stop with appreciation. Desire is involved, and with desire there is usually arousal. How dangerous or disruptive this may be depends on the individual who is doing the observing, but beauty in this instance cannot be considered in a vacuum. It has an effect, and the effect is not risk-free, morally speaking. Whether this is dangerous or not depends on the values and actions of the observer, but it is and will always be a consideration.

One other way in which a man may become obsessed with a particular woman is to consider her a muse of sorts, a presence that seems always beyond him while being simultaneously near, a love that is unfulfilled and unfulfillable but indispensable. One finds it in William Butler Yeats' "Song of the Wandering Angus." Angus catches a trout that turns into a "glimmering girl" who promptly vanishes. Angus spends the rest of his life searching for her in vain, but the search becomes his reason for living. In Arabic literature there is a character known as the Mujnoon Laila, who does the same, He searches and searches for Laila, also in vain, but he never gives up. The literal translation of Mujnoon is something close to madman. And then, of course, there is Dante Alighieri who was wounded so deeply by his brief sight of Beatrice that she became the basis of a new life (*La Vita Nuova*) and a symbol of sanctifying grace in *The Divine Comedy*. In this same vein a friend recently told me that John Clare was so possessed by his muse that he felt it was equal to the love he had for his wife. These obsessions (and that's what they really are) are disruptively "inspiring" because they attribute to women qualities that no woman could ever live up to. In this sense they are at heart romantic and are at odds with life itself. The mesmerizing effect of the young girl on the male admirer or "lover" transforms him forever. His life, to use the example of Dante, becomes "pre-Beatrice" and "post Beatrice." A disruptive experience has happened to him, and he can never be the same. But where would he or any of us be without beauty in our lives, regardless of danger?

Since I have already stressed a similarity between beauty and love, I could just as easily ask what would our lives be without love? My answer is that we would be just as mortally impoverished without love in our lives as we would be if deprived of beauty. Both are essential. Consider for a moment the alternative—a purely functional existence governed solely by what is needed to survive, i.e., food, water, shelter etc. These sustain us physically only. Instead of being capable of being moved or inspired, we would simply be employed, housed, fed, clothed and, in the parlance of the trade, informed. All of this is without transcendence. In contemporary societies the need to be informed is thought of as the epitome of a complete and worthwhile civic life. We are not stopped or elevated above the moment, however momentarily, as we might be while listening to Ravel or reading a sonnet of Shakespeare or studying the street corners in Paris that Caillebotte painted. On the contrary we are so buried under the burden of endless information that we are unable to rise above it to gain the perspective we need as beauty-impoverished human beings.

Any beautiful object (or sound, etc.) actuates our imaginations. A work of art in any medium awakens the latent imaginative power in all of us. One does not merely hear a beautiful song or tone poem; one absorbs it until one's entire self is one with it. And the experience is not easily (or ever) forgotten. Moreover, whether we realize it or not, we are changed however slightly by the experience.

To some that it is blessing. To others it is a danger. Fundamentalists, dogmatists, advocates of thought control, dictators, censors and rigorous moralists who are self-appointed defenders of public morality are often suspicious of and opposed to the arts for just that reason.

Attempts to suppress, demonize or otherwise denigrate the beautiful in our lives for whatever reason—pseudo-religious, political or otherwise—are eventually futile for the simple reason that suppressing the indispensable is against a natural law. Like freedom, beauty, once experienced, prevents the one who experienced it from returning to his former condition. Small wonder then that poets and artists are among the first to be tried, imprisoned or murdered when totalitarians rule. Creators of beauty remind us of those resources that repressive societies fear most.

Big Numbers, Small Print, Smooth Talk, Bad Results

In 2009, the cost of one Stealth bomber was $1,157,000,000. Repeat: one billion one hundred and fifty-seven million. One plane. By way of comparison the total current annual budget for the National Endowment for the Arts is $155,000,000. The cost of a single Stealth bomber is approximately eight times that number, which means that the current total of dollars allocated for the arts throughout the country would probably be able to offset the cost of the landing gear or part of the wing of one Stealth bomber. If proof by statistics and history is offensive or not persuasive to you, you should stop reading now. But if you take numerical and historic data seriously as a way of reaching unavoidable conclusions, then you're welcome to read on.

The federal outlay for what is termed defense (the military services plus the attendant manufacturers of aircraft, ships, tanks, vehicles etc.) constitutes almost a fourth of the 3.107 trillion national budget. The yearly outlay for the arts is less than one percent—.005%; the cost per taxpayer is something close to thirty-five cents (.35) a year. (In Canada and Sweden, both with smaller population than ours, the outlay for the arts is 10%.) For further documentation of money allocated and spent for "defense," consider the following, The cost of the ongoing war in Iraq (long since proved and judged illegal, misguided and unnecessary by everyone except its initiators and those profiting from it) has been calculated at $5,000 per second. This translates into $300,000 per minute, which when multiplied by the number of minutes in an hour totals $18,000,000. Keep multiplying, and you find that the war costs $412,000,000 a day. This eventually leads you to the neighborhood of $150,000,000,000 a year. These ongoing war costs are extraordinary as well as indefensible except to say that they are meant to protect our troops in combat situations in which they should never have been involved. But multiply the aforementioned annual cost of the war by the number of years we have been in Iraq, and you begin to see that the cost contributes mightily to the deficit, which in turn shrinks the economy, which in turn impacts the private and corporate foundations that no longer are able to support the arts as they would like. The result is that one arts organization after another disappears. This is where we find ourselves at the moment.

Senator George McGovern, who not only was a long-time elected official but had a doctorate in history, agreed with many others, that we are over-weaponized, conventionally and nuclearly. And years before McGovern made this statement, President Eisenhower presciently warned against the growing power of the military-industrial complex. Since then that complex has only grown stronger. And because weapons and war machinery exist for use in war and grow obsolete when not used, is it too brazen to ask if the military-industrial complex nudged recent administrations toward war as a kind of answer. The Vietnam War, called a mistake by its very architects (McGeorge Bundy and Robert McNamara) and similarly branded by a younger and more candid John Kerry ("How do you ask a man to be the last man to die for a mistake?") cost the lives of 58,220 Americans alone. For what? Similarly in Iraq, there was no initial justification, and all those who now say it was for democracy and not for oil and the security of Israel need a refresher course in *real politique.* And then there is the widely disseminated sentence of late former Secretary of State Madeline Albright: "Why do we have a military if we don't use it?" The chairman of the Joint Chiefs of Staff and the President of Boeing could not have said it better. But waging war for the sake of war has never been a true American ideal, and plunging the country into war for underlying industrial reasons is something that leaders do at their peril. And yet it seems habitual that men with third-rate minds continue to send first-rate volunteers to fight and die or be maimed in fifth-rate wars. "Serial wars" is what David Bromwich called them.

And look at the tawdry and jejune group of "warriors" and their stewards and lawyers who have led us to this impasse—a former President and Vice-President, the draft-evading neo-cons like Elliott Abrams and the rest. It remains inexplicable why President Obama, who is steeped in law, did not vigorously "go where the evidence leads." The statute of limitations has not expired. If justice delayed is justice denied, then injustice ignored is injustice absolved. Forget magnanimity. Vice-President Cheney publicly has continued to defend the illegal practice of torture after one professional interrogator after another has testified to its immorality as well as its unreliability. And lawyers have stressed that testimony gained through torture is inadmissible in court. But Cheney goes on unchecked, and Simon & Schuster has given him a six-figure advance to continue his crusade in print. And this is the same man who ducked service four times in a Vietnam War in which he deeply believed, saying, "I had other priorities." This creed almost rhymes with that of another "true believer." It was Newt Gingrich who used as his excuse, "I thought I could serve my country better in the future." How's that for statesmanship?

All this profligacy and cowardice and hypocrisy is a matter of dishonorable record. But what does it say about us as a people? Shall we continue to suffer the consequences of all this lethal folly while ignoring or strangling those human energies that give us art, drama, literature, dance, music and poetry? These are the forms of expression that should first and foremost become us as a country and of which they are the deserved and deserving crown. What else but the arts confirm our right to feel what we feel? What else but the arts are capable of showing us who we really are? War, even when it is regrettably necessary, has as its legacy suffering, death and waste. To bring the point home, imagine the difference between war and peace as the difference between a fist and a hand. A fist is fit for punching, nothing more. A hand can, among other things, write, paint, sculpt, create music from instruments and, in doing so, inspire and heal. Of the two uses of the hand, which performs the more beneficial human act?

In the meanwhile, what has become of us as a previously identified open society? Air travel has the same disconcerting flavor that one tastes when one makes an annual visit to a dentist. One hopes for a clean bill but is often confronted with the need for subsequent visits to attend to this and that. The job of screeners at our airports is the same—to root about for anything suspicious. Of course, it is small consolation when check-ups by government agents reveal that these same agents were able to board aircraft with lethal weapons on their persons or in their hand luggage that went through security undetected. The same often holds true for checkpoints at government buildings and at various buildings in the private sector. Convincing arguments have been and can be made for the necessity of pre-emptive measures (and I do not take them for granted), but the effect of these on our social lives is to make them more cramped, sour and overcast with the fog of suspicion. Moreover, it has made Security Incorporated a big and highly profitable business.

Little by little we have developed a Maginot mentality. For months before the invasion of France by Nazi Germany, the French believed that they would be protected by a line of protective trenches and forts on their eastern front. They became imprisoned and mesmerized by a sense of security that the Maginot Line offered them. In many ways we resemble the French—not in terms of dealing with an imminent threat but in the belief that our various security measures will insulate us from danger.

What about our way of life as we live and move and breathe in this cocoon of presumed security? Are we just going through the motions of normal civilian life? The televised news programs are just a breath away, if that, from packaged entertainment interspersed with sales pitches. What passes for patriotism is an affront to patriotism—lapel pins, bumper stickers, flags snapping from car antennae, bicep or buttocks tattoos, souped-up versions of the national anthem at sports events and the tagline of "God bless America" at the conclusion of speeches whose shallowness insults both God and America. The militarization of our daily vocabulary has long been noted since the end of World War II. We are prone to "attack problems." We declare "War on Poverty." One wonders if we would be just as willing to declare "War on War." In the name of patriotism and security the level of public discourse becomes more adulterated by the day. One public official even went to the extreme of stating that French Fries should be re-christened Freedom Fries because the French had the temerity of not siding with us before and during the illegal and lethal invasion of Iraq. But this was merely the inevitable consequence of a presidential pronouncement that labeled all who were not "with us" as being "against us."

American culture in the past has shown that it is simply better than this.

Civility in discourse, disturbingly absent from much of what passes for public discussion and debate of late, was once the identifying norm for what debate should be. Humor now has been sharpened into satire by and large. The happy humor of clowns finds a limited audience, proving that we have somehow lost our capacity for mirth. Newspaper journalism is not now what it once was, not only because there are fewer and fewer newspapers, but because personal animus has replaced the more reliable pursuit of facts that should ultimately be left to speak for themselves.

In retrospect we cannot forget that Richard Nixon carried every state but Massachusetts in 1972 and that George W. Bush, though "elected" in 2000 by Judge Scalia and four associates, was, to the utter dismay of our closest allies in Europe and Latin America, re-elected in 2004. In the face of all this open mendacity and skullduggery, we waxed indignant. We elected a new president in the hope that conditions as we have known them will be reversed or at least identified for all to see as the cause of our indignation. One of the things that has been disturbingly evident since 2000 is that indignation in the face of arrogance has often been the loser. Arrogance has proceeded on its merry way. And when that happened, we retreated from indignation and even rage into indifference.

And that is our problem to solve. Will we embrace the spirit of the original American Revolution and summarily demand that we live by our constitutional ideals? Or will we make an initial attempt and then, either through impatience or weakness in the face of opposition, lapse into indifference again?

A Love Like No Other

All genuine love stories have moments of joy as well as moments of sadness. They may vary in intensity or duration, but they are never absent. Those who think of love as uninterrupted joy are romantics. Those who are obsessed only with sadness deserve their misery.

This love story came to me out of coincidence. In the 1950s I met George when we were both quartered in Quantico with other newly commissioned second lieutenants in the Marine Corps. We became friends. He told me that he was a Yale graduate and that he intended to return to his home in Oakland, California, and establish his own business. And he did, becoming one of the most prominent corporate executives in California. I learned from newsletters created and forwarded by some of our fellow alumni that he was married and had several children. Then in 2002, we met on the occasion of the 50th reunion of our class, learning that three had been killed, that two had "stayed in" and become generals, that Karl Ullrich had served as Director of Athletics at Annapolis and then at West Point and that Pete Soderberg was the father of Steven Soderberg, an award-wining Hollywood director, screenwriter and actor.

George was late arriving at the reunion. I recognized him instantly because he had changed little. We had a warm greeting, although I detected a certain sadness in him. A day later we had time together after dinner, and I told him as tactfully as I could that he looked as if something was bothering him. He paused and said that his wife had died less than a month before. He then added that it was not his first wife—the one he married after he left the Marine Corps. He said that they had had several children, but she came to him suddenly one day and told him she did not want to be married anymore and left. From then on, he and his wife became legally separated, and he raised his children to adulthood while maintaining his prospering business interests.

One evening in his middle 60s, he invited an associate to a theatrical performance in San Francisco. He had purchased two choice tickets and was waiting in a lobby guest room for the associate to arrive. Others were also waiting, including a woman who looked both mature and young. Finally, the room emptied, except for the woman and George. A few moments before the show was due to start, George approached her and said, "Excuse me, but are you waiting for the same reason that I am?" She smiled and explained that her guest had not arrived as well. George nodded and then, ignoring his usual prudence, asked, "Would you like to see the show with me? I have two excellent tickets, and seeing this show solo would be like having dinner alone." She smiled quizzically as if in agreement. In short, they saw the show and thoroughly enjoyed their time together. George invited the woman, Betty, to dinner in San Francisco twice after that. The second dinner was even more satisfying than the first. They discussed authors (John Updike) and places (Paris) and actors (Spencer Tracy, Eva Marie Saint) they mutually admired. For a week, George re-lived and re-relished those evenings before he telephoned her again. A woman answered the phone, and George asked her if he could speak to Betty.

"Who is calling?" the woman asked.

"George. She'll recognize my name."

After a pause the woman said with emphasis, "Betty does not want to see or speak to you again."

"Pardon me?"

"She does not want you to call her again," the woman added and hung up.

For several days George thought about nothing but that. Finally, he called back. The same woman answered. She said nothing, but she remained on the line while George pleaded with her to explain her—and Betty's—rejection. At last, the woman explained that she was Betty's sister. She went on to say that Betty had been seriously injured while lifting her nephew at the beach weeks earlier. Somehow what she thought was a mere sprain turned out to be damage to her spinal cord, and the result was that she could no longer walk. George asked if he could speak to Betty. There was a pause, and the next voice he heard was Betty's. She said she appreciated his call, that she was beginning to learn to accept her condition, that she did not want sympathy and that he should forget that he ever met her.

A month after the call, George damaged his Achilles tendon while playing tennis. On crutches for weeks, he finally decided to call Betty and tell her they now had similar handicaps and that it might help them both if they shared their misery. She yielded. They met regularly at her home.

Months later during a routine medical exam, it was discovered that Betty had a treatable liver cancer. When she told George about the diagnosis, she did not have any idea what his response would be. There was an interval of silence, and then George proposed and insisted that they should be married.

"Who would want to marry a crippled woman with cancer?" Betty asked.

"I would," said George.

They indeed were married and had four years together before Betty died. George told me that he and Betty somehow learned to dance together and even had sexual relations. He never went into detail on either of these subjects, and I never intruded.

It became more and more apparent to me, and later George confirmed, that he regarded these few years with Betty as the happiest years of his life, and her death devastated him. Knowing of my interest in poetry, he told me that Betty wrote poetry. He showed me one of her poems that he included in her funeral service, and it summarized and said everything.

Warm May afternoon sun
behind the oak tree.
Chime and leaf-rustling breeze.
How peacefully I love you.

Why the Religious Right Is Religiously Wrong

Why have so few said that the current preoccupation of the Religious Right with faith and politics is simplistic to the point of folly? The faith in question here is a dehydration of Christianity that presents itself as if the Renaissance and the Reformation had never happened. Its bedrock is a literal belief in Biblical texts not open to disquisition or question. This includes and even forcefully emphasizes the Apocalypse of John, which is made synonymous with expectations of the "rapture" and the inevitable Armageddon where the world presumably will come to a nuclear end. However over-simplified this synopsis of such fundamentalism may appear, the fact remains that it has been embraced by millions of "true believers." And the politicization of this army of believers has been exploited and militarized by ultra-conservative and neo-conservative operators to the point where people like Pat Robertson and Jerry Falwell and their various emulators were actually regarded by some as prophets. Forget for the moment, if you can, the latent anti-Semitism in their belief that the Jews will be gathered at the time of the Second Coming (presumably in Israel) and face conversion or death. Forget as well the impressive commercial dimensions of these evangelistic movements. Forget too such forerunners as Oral Roberts, Jimmy Swaggart and Jim and Tammy Faye Bakker. They were all replicas of one another, and their joint message was repent, pray and pay.

The pathos of all this is that these evangelical operators have assumed a kind of sacral position in public life. Their views are frequently solicited on serious questions of the day, particularly by Fox and similar cable networks. They are invited to preside at state or national functions, and they often are photographed with heads of state. Their militancy is, shall we say, non-denominational, and they run in a direct historical line from Cotton Mather to William Jennings Bryan to Father Divine to Charles Coughlin to other Elmer Gantrys of more recent vintage. In fact, this is a strain in Christianity that surfaced in the second century after Christ. For every Minicius Felix who could face adversity and say philosophically, "Is it not foolish to worship what one ought to weep for, and weep for what one ought to worship," there was always a Tertullian who proclaimed that the flesh and the spirit were at constant war, and this was but a metaphor for our lives on this planet.

Acting as if the Renaissance and Reformation had no effect historically on matters of faith and thought is to deny the very flowering of Western culture. It is not without some justification that the centuries prior to the Renaissance were known as the Dark Ages. After all, to live the life of the living dead in anticipation of the Second Coming (always considered imminent) was to absolve oneself *a priori* of the responsibilities of personal growth and social involvement. If the world could end at any moment, according to this worldview, why bother to exert efforts on behalf of life and growth at all? Far wiser, say these people, to prepare oneself for eternal judgment and wait, even though the preparation and waiting period might be lifelong. Strains of such a mentality are alive and well today, as I learned some years back while driving from Midland, Texas, to Abilene. I turned on the radio of the rental car I was driving to relieve the monotony of the trip. Between programs dealing with cattle prices and the gospel hymns of one Brother Benjamin, I was surprised to learn that Jesus Christ was due to appear at a specific street corner in Dallas on the following morning. This was a brief comic respite from what I still regard as the most boring of drives, but it attested to the fact that Bible Belt dogmatism was alive and well in north-central Texas. What such true believers not only ignore but miss entirely is how Christian humanism finally triumphed over the prophets of doom—even though it took centuries for this to happen. If the world is seen as a vale of tears or a pre-incubation period where the elect are chosen and marked for salvation even before they die, then what many people call our very lives are nothing but delays for rewards to come for the Elect. But it wasn't until the humanists of Europe rebelled against this simplistic view of salvation that Christian life in its cultural dimensions began to develop. The Miracle and Morality Plays, for example, despite their inherent didacticism, eventually evolved into the apogee of Elizabethan drama. It gave us Marlowe, Beaumont, Fletcher, Jonson and, triumphantly, William Shakespeare. In education the works of Ascham, Linacre, Erasmus and Thomas More opened the mind to more than the merely doctrinaire. And at the same time similar developments were happening in music, art and architecture, and all of these advances were to become the bedrock of Western culture.

In effect, the undergirding of this cultural renaissance was a re-discovery of the ancient texts of Plato, Aristotle, Plotinus, Galen, Euclid and Archimedes—texts that Muslim Arabs and Sephardic Jews in Moorish Spain saved from total loss by translating them into Arabic, from which they were subsequently translated into the vernaculars of Europe. One historian has called "these books the most important documentary discovery (or 're-discovery') in Western intellectual history." And he is absolutely correct. Moreover, if the two dominant influences on Christianity are what Matthew Arnold called Hebraism and Hellenism, it was the re-discovery of the classics that provided the impetus. Men began to realize that their lives in this world were not meant to be static but dynamic and that pagan authors could and indeed had provided the seminal works on politics, ethics, mathematics, poetics, astronomy and medicine that made life more than a stoic preparation for death.

Fundamentalists of all stripes have chosen to ignore or belittle this while ironically benefiting from a culture that Renaissance thought made possible. This goes a long way toward explaining their militancy, their messianic habit of mind, their impatience with doubt and their almost complete lack of humility. His biographers claim that Ronald Reagan accepted the view that Armageddon was proximate, but he was adroit enough to conceal it from the electorate with affability. George W. Bush, lacking Reagan's adroitness, personified the aforementioned fundamentalism almost to the letter—messianic, militant, undoubting and arrogant. If such qualities of character result from daily readings from the Bible, which Bush said he did, then the best advice for Mr. Bush would be that he diversify his reading.

The Hebraistic influence upon Christianity was and remains longitudinal. It stressed man's relationship with God. The Hellenistic influence was latitudinal, emphasizing man's relationship with other men and with the natural world. This was what occupied Aristotle's attention. The world and the men in it were not to be ignored or renounced but respected and understood. "To Aristotle," wrote Richard E. Rubinstein, "the good life always meant living happily in the present world rather than renouncing pleasures for the sake of eternal bliss. Moderation as opposed to extremes of asceticism or sensuality was his watchword. Friendship, family life, political participation and study ('contemplation') were the keys to genuine happiness—a view that may seem quite conventional now, but one that caused great consternation when his ethical works were rediscovered centuries later by Christians with their hopes fixed on heaven."

One of the unpleasant ruptures that results when Christianity in its most fundamental form has to deal with Aristotelian humanism is abolitionism or worse. In the earliest centuries of Christianity, the Manicheans set the body against the spirit with disastrous results. It took Church Councils and Thomas Aquinas to straighten out the mess caused. Centuries later the *Reconquista* (re-conquest) of Andalusian

Spain offered a more catastrophic example of abolitionism. In this war of ethnic cleansing in order to re-Catholicize Spain, the forces of Fernando and Isabella drove the Muslims and Jews from Andalusia. What came to an end was eight centuries during which Muslims, Christians and Jews under Muslim governance created one of the rarest and richest of civilizations where people of three faiths lived in mutual respect. The three sects served to fertilize one another's creativity in literature, music and architecture in ways not seen before or since. This all ended when the Muslims and Jews who survived the battles were faced with death, exile or forcible conversion, and the result was an impoverishment of Spain for centuries. This can be cited as a prototype of what can happen to a society—*any* society—when triumphalism replaces creative civility. Such triumphalism may be vicious or simply sophomoric, as in the idiotic denigration of France and all matters French when the French government cast its UN vote against the Bush administration's push for a vote of approval for its planned invasion of Iraq. In its usual form, however, it reduces everything to "He who is not with Me is against Me."

Coming from the mouth of Christ Himself, this presents no real problem. Coming from the mouth of one or more of His followers ("You're either with us or against us"), it seems the height of presumption, especially when it is said as a veiled threat with severe consequences. One reason for this is that giving someone an either/or choice assumes that one alternative is all-good and its opposite all-bad. In human relations such clarity rarely prevails, and the righteous vindictiveness done to coerce compliance is repugnant by nature. Robespierre said that "no one likes an armed missionary." And who was it wrote that crimes and violence done in the name of religion are more numerous historically than crimes and violence done against religion itself? The aforementioned Spanish Inquisition is perhaps the most glaring historical example, but witch-burners in New England, deranged murderers seemingly ordered by God to kill in His name, and zealots who throw the stones of denigration and slander at dissenters still rank high on such a list.

Trying to impose doctrinaire visions upon political life, as Tom DeLay vowed to do before he was defrocked of his role as the Republican "hammer" in the House, is a formula for havoc. Although freedom of worship is one of the fundamental Constitutional guarantees in American society, the framers never went so far as to specify which religions would be acceptable and which not. And they were insistent on the separation of church and state. The divinity that Jefferson named in the Declaration of Independence was essentially one that could be adduced by human reason alone, which is recognized by scholastics as theodicy. It results in Deism. But democracy and theologies of any kind were seen as incompatible. When President Eisenhower was asked about the importance of faith in American public life, he answered that he believed in belief, and he left it at that. And that was a statement with which Jefferson would have agreed.

Although American Presidents to date have been Christians from various denominations, the unlikely assumption can be made that a Jew, Muslim, Hindu or even an agnostic could somehow be elected. But the dictum of separation of church and state would still prevail. Fundamentalists of any faith would be confronted with the same stiffening resistance that the current Religious Right is facing today. And for good reason. The righteous autocrat is finally unwelcome in American politics. Citizens are not subjects. They cannot and will not be governed by pronouncements but by plausible arguments that must be persuasive to 51% of the electorate to become operative. Religious fanatics who attempt to coerce compliance by intimidation or pressure of various kinds do as much damage to the body politic at the most vital level as do those connivers who "fix" or otherwise steal elections. They totally block rational discourse. They make civility impossible. They also demonstrate a regrettable sterility of imagination. It is evident, for example, in their distrust of the arts, and their inclination to think in apocalyptic terms. Debate becomes a fight for supremacy. Naked force is condoned as a justifiable means if the ends are regarded as justifiable. And the result inevitably is confusion followed by rationalization, which is the usual recourse for all who do not think before they leap.

It was Thornton Wilder who wrote that "violence is the result of a failure of imagination." We see the evidence around us every day in one congressional, presidential or military debacle after another, in deceptive speech-making, in policies that condone the torture and alleged murder of prisoners, etc. Moreover, the cultural poverty of the Religious Right becomes more and more evident in their almost total lack of introspection, self-correction and admission (or even recognition) of error. Their reliance on direct statement is commendable, but only if it leads to clarity. When it becomes a synonym for evasion or venom with righteous overtones, it's disastrous. And if it is accompanied by a scornful boldness, it becomes obnoxious and even criminal. Yet they nonetheless have the temerity to say they speak in God's name while, as one author has perceptively written, the true God sits in heaven like a fool.

War as Pornography

One of the key essays in Susan Sontag's *Style of Radical Will* (1966) was entitled "The Pornographic Imagination." The most memorable lines for me were: "What difficulties arise (related to sexuality) come from the long deformation of the sexual impulse by Western Christianity, whose ugly wounds virtually everyone in this culture bears. First, guilt and anxiety. Then the reduction of sexual capacities—leading if not to virtual impotence and frigidity, at least to the depletion of sexual energy and the regression of many natural elements of sexual appetite. Then the spill-over into public dishonesties in which people tend to respond to news of the sexual pleasures of others with envy, fascination, revulsion and spiteful indignation. It's from this pollution of the sexual health of the culture that a phenomenon like pornography is derived."

Historically much of this deformation in the United States was traceable to the influence of Jansenism, particularly, though not exclusively, on American Catholicism. This version of Jansenism was inclined to impute evil or "impurity" to the sexual appetite as such. This created among unquestioning believers and some parents the view that almost anything that provoked sexual desire was sinful in itself or could easily become an "occasion of sin." The primary defense against such provocations was repudiation through distraction, penitential practices, prayer and so on. Often this only made the denier more vulnerable to the very appetites that he or she was denying. At this point what filled the void created by the suppression and enticed by curiosity was often pornography. "What pornography does," Sontag adds later in the same essay, "is precisely to drive a wedge between one's existence as a free human being and one's existence as a sexual being—while in ordinary life a healthy person is one who prohibits such a gap from opening up."

It takes little imagination to see that demonizing the sexual appetite and separating it from the "total person" would leave the follower of such a mindset both sexually curious and vulnerable to whatever might present itself as a solution. This is what gives pornography all the opening it needs to appear as a makeshift, though crude, solution. It did this initially in art (even prehistorical cave art), spoken or printed language, dramatic action and eventually in pictorial magazines and film.

At present, film serves the purposes of pornography more effectively than language. Even the graphic wall paintings that were discovered on the brothel walls of Pompeii and Herculaneum seem amateurish compared to what's accessible on film or YouTube. Regardless of subject matter, modern cinematography shows all there is to see from a distance or closeup, but the result is that what's seen becomes more and more impersonal. This is possibly what prompted Margaret Mead to say definitively that pornography is sexuality divorced from personality. Regardless, pornography in all its manifestations does have an audience in the United States that grows by the year. A recent survey revealed that the annual income from pornography in the United States was approximately $15,000,000,000, which exceeds the annual profits of ABC, NBC and CBS combined.

Leaving economic assets aside as unrelated to the purpose of this essay, it should be evident to any dispassionate observer that pornography is the enemy of personality. While love in its truest form is unifying, pornography disrupts. It tantalizes with promises of pleasure disassociated from love and kindness and patience although sexuality can only become its destined self when it is most intimate, personal and private, i.e. when sustained by love, kindness and patience. Nobel awardee Octavio Paz expressed this pointedly in what is probably the best book written on the subject of love (*The Double Flame*) that is chosen freely by a man and a woman—conjugal love. He said that such love is the final metaphor for sexuality in marriage since it is the mutual and tangible expression through the body of what is known in the soul. "Every love," Paz concluded, "is eucharistic." John Donne in his poem "The Ecstasie" said the same thing centuries earlier when he wrote, "Love's mysteries in souls do grow/but yet the body is his book." However spiritual the love between a man and a woman may be, it expresses and fulfills itself through the body, i.e. eucharistically.

Historically there are two traditions that have emerged as the natural enemies of eucharistic love. In his classic work, *Love in the Western World*, on this subject, the internationally recognized Swiss author Denis de Rougemont traces them to Don Juan and Tristan.

For Don Juan there was never one woman to love and be loved by but any female of the species to be seduced, possessed and abandoned. For Don Juan, love was fundamentally an appetite to be satisfied at will when aroused. The impersonality of this desire in his case makes it possible and logical to detect parallels with the essence of pornography itself.

Tristan, on the other hand, loved Isolde and only Isolde. Because she was married, he knew that his love for her could never be fulfilled. The result was that he idolized a woman he could never marry. His sublimation of his condition led him to revere and even idolize her. As a man of arms, he came to regard his profession as an alternate outlet for his sexual passion. Since only death could release him from the agony of his unfulfillable life, he and many courtly lovers like him gave knighthood and the profession of arms a romantic dimension because it was their way of daring death with the love for a sacrosanct woman as their motivation. It ennobled them. It created an opportunity for them to display what they regarded as their essential masculinity through the profession of arms.

Both the traditions of Don Juan and Tristan are based on passion—both when relieved or denied. Both are not the love that Octavio Paz identified as eucharistic. But de Rougemont takes the consequences and implications of passionate love in the character and tradition of Tristan a step further. While Plutarch regarded passion as morbid, and Menander saw it as ridiculous excess, de Rougemont identifies passion as one of the major motivators of action in the modern world. Passion goes beyond reason in many instances and becomes its own justification. It can even become the core of nationalism and romanticism. After he became anathema to the Nazis before and during World War II, de Rougemont noted how Hitler relied on "hypnotic passion and not reflection" in his speeches. This created a "collective hypnosis." Hitler used this hypnosis through oratory, *sieg heil* salutes and colossal rallies to make the population subservient to his will. Trump strove through rallies and incessant social media onslaughts to create the same hypnosis, but in 2020 the upsurge of democracy created a majority of Americans who thankfully voted to reject it. It was truly a great moment in American history although the continued defiance of Trumpers and their likenesses cannot ever be ignored.

It is this hypnosis that is the sustainer and expander of the pornography of war. You see it in the training of soldiers as they march in lockstep and shout rousing cheers as they march. You hear it in the pep talk of politicians as they begin sloganeering the one-liners that their followers perpetuate verbatim. All of such habits are not only part and parcel of this "collective hypnosis" but are the enemies of individual thought and action. I have already noted how pornography, particularly visual pornography, is capable of arousing those affected by it to be dominated by passion until that passion is satisfied. In the same sense a frustrated but aroused passion like Tristan's for Isolde can become a way of inspiring those so frustrated to let it become their motivation for heroism in battle. As Americans we are caught up in the same tradition. The chivalric nature of our conduct in wars to date does reveal that the country being defended does seem to have a woman's soul for which our deeds in war were done. This delusion is what conceals or disguises the brutality and havoc of war in all its viciousness.

One of the demands of hypnotized populations is their need to find an enemy on whom they can project their dissatisfactions. Hitler gave it to his followers by exploiting their racial consciousness and demanding *lebensraum*. That was a preface to the war that eventually followed. George W. Bush was to lie about non-existent chemical weapons in Iraq (as did General Colin Powell) in order to initiate his "war on terror." A more impersonal war-slogan could not have been imagined, but it was sufficiently fungible to be imputed to anyone who could be considered an enemy. It was a prolongation of a tired tactic that was used in Vietnam before it became obvious that defeating an indigenous people in their own country would not accommodate such a formula. We even created a slogan whose audacity contained the seeds of its own defeat—we were going to "Vietnamize the Vietnamese." The same audacity is on display with slogans like "Operation Iraqi Freedom" and the like. It all comes down to passion without sense, which is political pornography defined. Such pornography makes wars possible and continues to justify them while they are being waged. The cost in American lives in presidentially chosen wars from 1950 to the present is in the tens of thousands. The number of wounded and displaced is incalculable ("We don't count the enemy.") What's hidden by war's arithmetic is an ultimate pornography that war makes possible—the murder of designated enemies either at close quarters or from a distance by bullet, bomb or fire. Bodies are blown apart in ways that make identification impossible. Flags, parades, close-order drill and spotless uniforms become mere formalities compared to the dirty but chosen business of battle where total strangers murder total strangers in the ultimate pornography for which they have been trained.

The romanticization of war that makes this palatable has a complete archive of assets. It canonizes men like Sergeant York and Commando

Kelly and others in terms of "kills" credited to them. I do not mean this as a disparagement of York and Kelly, but the highest and most revered of awards in our country is the Congressional Medal of Honor, which is given in recognition of altruism. Those to whom it is given (often posthumously) had to have performed an act of uncommon bravery for the sake of someone else and, had they not placed themselves in jeopardy, no one could blame them. The humanity of that speaks for itself.

War in our time results in innumerable deaths. The consummate propaganda of war's pornography invariably begets and sustains and attempts to justify such wars. This is why the initiators of war work tirelessly to make them appear altruistic or patriotic to the public as well as to the armed forces. War propaganda is governed almost exclusively by this theme, which essentially is the arousing pornography that masks the inevitability of violent death, disfigurement or dismemberment. Soldiers and others, although trained to kill, are not said to go to war to kill but to save, to free, to preserve. This has a history that goes back to Trojan War. The legend has it that Helen was abducted by Paris, the son of King Priam of Troy, and that the Greeks went to war against Troy to return Helen to her husband Menelaus. The alternate version has it that Helen eloped with Paris or at least was a happy abductee. Paris was young and handsome compared to the braggart she married. The Greeks would go to war to save a ruler's kidnapped wife but not one who loved her kidnapper. Underlying this personal story was the fact that Troy controlled the Dardanelles, and that such control permitted it to determine who would and would not be allowed to sail through the Dardanelles and trade at ports in the Sea of Marmora and the Black Sea. The Greeks knew that defeating Troy in a war would guarantee them such access, but the war had to be seen as inevitable and noble. The happily kidnapped Helen provided the plausible lie that the Greeks were going to war for the sake and honor of Helen, and it worked.

When dangers or ambitions widen into wars, what worked at Troy still works. Updated in different but recognizable ways, Troy lives again wherever there's a war although the "historical Troy" is no longer on the map. And the ideal of "saving Helen" lives as well, even though Helen is known by other names.

No More Love Letters

I have always been amused by Hollywood's vision of writers at work. The writer is presented seated at a desk on which sits a typewriter or a computer. Suddenly the writer seems inspired and begins typing feverishly. The camera stays on him as he continues to type, and his manuscript grows page by page into a neat stack on the desk. The scene is impressive but bogus.

Most writers—and I'm speaking as a writer and as one acquainted with other writers—write spontaneously. By that I mean that they do not write at a specific time every day. Writing is a much more volatile and unpredictable calling. It might begin when the writer scrawls on a sheet of paper or the back of an envelope a phrase or a word that is for him provocative. Later it might evolve into a complete paragraph. It is rarely willed into being but takes shape gradually from a germinal insight or image. Such insights often tarry until they choose to reveal themselves in their entirety at a time of their choosing. This is why writing and waiting to write are one and the same thing for all true writers. Inspiration dissipates when forced or willed into expression.

Since writing happens in one sense because the writer "can't get out of it," there is invariably something totally original in a writer's first drafts. They are usually written by hand and eventually evolve into the final typed or printed versions. But it is the original versions that are seminal. This is why first drafts and notes are prized so highly even after the final versions are completed. They show how the evolution from drafts and sketches to the final work happened. They explain to some extent the evolution of the creative process.

Now that the art (and it is an art in that it is something made by hand) of handwriting (or cursive) is being taught less and less, one wonders what if anything will take its place. When I asked my grandson years ago if handwriting was being taught in his school, he said, "No, they say we don't need it." What my grandson was not told was that there is a vital difference between a handwritten word and a word punched out on a keyboard. The latter simply does not have the "feel" of the essence of language. And this even has a physiological explanation. I recently read and copied from a medical textbook why this is so: "Writing with just the index finger rather than the whole hand no longer stimulates the neurons or the same cortical areas." In other words, there seems to be an undeniable connection between a hand-held pen or pencil and what is in the mind and heart. This explains the difference between mere wordage and "felt speech."

I suspect that the preference of a growing majority for the typed or printed word instead of the handwritten one reveals the triumph of communication over what I would define as communion. A typed-out message on a smartphone or a computer is basically a messaging of information; it is invariably one-dimensional, and all that is demanded of it is clarity and accuracy. A handwritten letter or a poem is primarily intended to convey feeling or felt thought. And the expression of such feelings or felt thoughts is universally regarded as language at its most memorable. This distinction between print and script prompted me to ask a number of different people—men and women—the same question, i.e., "Would you rather receive a love letter or a note of appreciation or good will emailed or handwritten?"

The answer from men tended to be frank but still casual. "Print is easier for me to read." "I have trouble reading most people's handwriting, so I would vote for the email." "What's the big problem? They both are saying the same thing, aren't they?"

The answers from women were unanimously in favor of the handwritten letter over the email, and the tone of their responses fluctuated between shock that such a question should even be asked and explaining the reasons for their preference in detail. "The answer to that is a no-brainer." "Are you joking? Anybody can use a machine." "A handwritten letter is more personal." "It's not what is said but how it is said that matters." "I throw away my emails. I'd never throw away a love letter. In fact, I keep all my love letters wrapped with a ribbon in a special drawer."

The answer that made the deepest impression on me did not require a single word. When I asked a young woman, who worked as a bank teller, if she would prefer a love letter written by hand or printed, she opened her purse, lifted out a fountain pen, bared the gold point and wrote her full name on a sheet of paper as if she were signing a marriage contract or a poem of her own. Rather than bother to give an answer, she let her perfect signature do it for her. And it did. And it still does whenever I think of it.

Facing the prospect that generations will never be taught to write by hand suggests to me not only the end of a genre but the likely end of heartfelt expression on paper by someone with a hand-held pen. Machine-generated statements can never match felt thoughts spoken by hand. Speeches and passionate letters penned by multiple authors are treasured for their authenticity in this regard. Misspellings and errors in punctuation or capitalization often make them even more valuable to collectors because they further accentuate the very humanity of the authors.

I have found that handwritten letters from soldiers in combat situations to their wives or families have the same veracity. Most memorably I learned that letters written by children to those dearest to them would disarm any skeptic. Decades ago, my wife was invited to accompany a group of bibliophiles to visit major libraries in Italy. Our son was under ten at the time, and the prospect of saying goodbye to his mother for almost two weeks did not exactly thrill him. After she was away for five days, I said that it might be a good idea "to call Mom." She was in Venice at the time, and, because of the time difference, my call reached her at five in the morning. "What's wrong?" she asked, alarmed. "Nothing's wrong," I answered. "We just wanted to hear your voice."

I turned to our son and offered him the phone, saying, "Do you want to say something to Mom?" He shook his head no and said he would write her a letter. He did and mailed it to the hotel in Venice. She received the forwarded letter two weeks after she returned from the trip. Our son had carefully written on a single page: "Dear Mom, I loved you before you left, I love you while you're away, and I'll love you when you come back. I have a little cold, but I think I'm getting better. Dad and I almost nearly can't get along without you."

I cannot find the adjective to describe how much that letter meant to her.

One Definite Mozart

Ever since I first began reading Richard Wilbur's poems in the late 1940's, I think I've read only one negative review of his work. It was not Randall Jarrell's somewhat patronizing critique of Wilbur's second book, *Ceremony*, but a review of *The Mind-Reader* by Calvin Bedient in *The New Republic* (June 5, 1976). Bedient contended that Wilbur was too safe a poet—that he rarely took chances. Bedient was not referring to subject matter; he was taking Wilbur to task for his deliberately choosing to remain within the limits of traditional metrics and prosody and yielding to "moral complacency."

I mention this now because one of my themes in this appreciation will be to demonstrate that Richard Wilbur's refreshing and refreshened traditionalisms along the lines of metrics and prosody are not a weakness but a strength and that "moral complacency" has nothing to do with that. And I make this statement as one not fully enthralled by that tradition as it is literally defined but fully supportive of Wilbur's achievements within it. To say smugly that Wilbur never took chances is to betray a superficial reading of Wilbur's work to date. The nuances of diversity and experiment are everywhere, and they serve to re-create rather than merely perpetuate the set patterns of quatrains, couplets, sonnets, pentameters, trimeters, or even the alliteratively linked linear segments that Wilbur adapted from the Anglo-Saxon scops.

That he has done so with almost Elizabethan elegance is what has distinguished his poetry among that of all his contemporaries from the time of the publication of The *Beautiful Changes* in 1947 to the appearance of *New and Collected Poems* in 1988, for which he received his second Pulitzer Prize, and finally to the most recent *Mayflies* in 2000 and a second collected edition in 2004. That he has been criticized by some who lack his consistent virtuosity within the chosen disciplines that he has embraced and with which he feels most comfortable is perhaps inevitable. But to me this is not unlike criticizing a tennis player for playing tennis (also an activity governed by fixed rules) exceptionally well on, of all things, a tennis court. Even if one does not like the game or the rules, one can at least respect the talent of one who has mastered them, re-created them in his own style and advanced and enriched the tradition by performing well within its strictures.

On the other hand, Calvin Bedient may simply not have been impressed by how a poem by Wilbur reads—how it evolves from the first word to the last. Those who believe that poetry is a mere stream of consciousness or that the language of poetry is nothing but the language of accidental associative meanings or that poetry is a kind of imaginative ink blot whose destiny is simply to expand itself to the limits of exhaustion will assuredly not read Richard Wilbur with pleasure. His work does not accommodate such frivolity. As a poet he has definite syllogistic way of thinking; his poems have a beginning, middle and an end that parallel the way we think from assertion to judgment. Not all of them follow the "If... but... therefore" mode of syllogistic logic, but a good many of them do, and the imprint of this way of thinking is characteristic of a mind that does not meander but concludes. Shakespeare's sonnets impress us with a similar way of thinking, which further accentuates my inclination to call Wilbur's style Elizabethan. Wilbur's poems seem to obey an inner imperative that is intellectual rather than emotional, or perhaps I should say emotionally intellectual. We sense that the poet is actually thinking through his feelings to their inevitable and ineluctable conclusion.

So much for preface and apologia. It is not my intent to defend Richard Wilbur against mere carping but to appreciate and admire his poetry that consistently rewards every moment of attention devoted to it. Rather than concentrate on Wilbur's evident technical virtuosity, I propose to focus on his artistic restraint, his genuine mirth, his sense of the tragic and his overall—for lack of a better word—felicity. By felicity I mean language that is happy with itself in the contexts that this poet has created for it. As a rule, Wilbur is such a felicitous poet except in those rare instances when he seems to be willing a poem into existence because something has aroused his indignation before his inspiration and talent can fully digest it.

To call Wilbur a formalist, as he has been called by many throughout his career, is simply to acknowledge that he writes within the established traditions of English and American poetics. But formalism is too pat a label to paste on any poet, and it clarifies little. The same could be said of Anthony Hecht or Stanley Kunitz, but so what? Isn't it more helpful to speak of Wilbur's restraint within his chosen formalisms, his peculiar aesthetic reserve that eschews the "let-it-all-hang-out" approach in favor of choosing the most minuscule detail that is capable of being the key to everything? For example, he does not flail blindly at the barbarism of war (which, as in infantryman in World War II, he must have seen at close quarters) but concentrates on a lonely sentry in "First Snow in Alsace" who is momentarily distracted by snow-swirls and snow-designs so that he ignores the whitening shell-holes, the snowdrifts on the ammunition stacks and, stunningly, the "snowfall (that) fills the eyes/Of soldiers dead a little while." Nor in another poem called "Place Pigalle" does he moralize about the whores and stripshows but somehow intermingles the lust and loneliness of soldiers on leave from the front who search out "their ancient friends" with the poignancy of a midsummer night's dream-like respite from a war that makes murderers out of young men who might otherwise be lovers:

"Ionized innocence: this pair reclines,
She on the table, he in a tilting chair,
With Arden ease; her eyes as pale as air
Travel his priestgoat face; his hand's thick tines
Touch the gold whorls of her Corinthian hair.

"Girl, if I love thee not, then let me die;
Do I not scorn to change my state with kings?
Your muchtouched flesh, incalculable, which wrings
Me so, now shall I gently seize in my
Desperate soldier's hands, which kill all things."

This poem illustrates Wilbur's restraint at its finest. The result is that the theme is strengthened by what is held back. I do not find this to be the case with "On the Eyes of an SS Officer," which ends with this explicit final stanza:

But this one's iced or ashen eyes devise,
Foul purities, in flesh their wilderness,
Their fire; I ask my makeshift God of this
My opulent bric-a-brac earth to damn his eyes.

The rhetoric of hatred is here, but the directness of its expression makes the poetry evaporate for me. Wilbur does not suffer such lapses often, but they do occur. Perhaps this is because his basic optimistic and open nature does not easily transmute rage and indignation into the stuff of poetry. Dante, of course, could do it. Neruda did it when his inspiration and indignation fused; otherwise, he simply versified a lot of personal bile and propaganda. Wilbur is capable of the right indignations, which means that he is outraged at the right times, but his moral umbrage often strips him of the restraint that is the fertile growing ground of his poetic talent. The difference is immediately noticeable in the aforementioned poem as well as in the concluding sestet of his "A Miltonic Sonnet for Mr. Johnson on His Refusal of Peter Hurd's Official Portrait."

> Rightly you say the picture is too large
> Which Peter Hurd by your appointment drew,
> And justly call that Capitol too bright
> Which signifies our people in your charge;
> Wait, Sir, and see how time will render you
> Who talk of vision but are weak of sight.

I suppose a case could be made for this poem as a re-creation of the Miltonic spirit in our time, but Wilbur's language has too direct an indebtedness to Milton for me to see it as anything more than an adaptation, despite the contemporaneity of the subject matter. The fact remains that Wilbur's formidable talent does not appear at its best when he is moved to write like this. It is not that one disagrees with his moral or political positions (agreement or disagreement is not relevant here) but with the way they are stated or rendered. Having known him more than casually for several decades, I would say that certain social or political issues affect him deeply and that he sincerely would like to take issue with guile or chicanery or plain wrongdoing through a poetic vision rather than through speeches, letters and the like. But such poems fail as poems more often than they succeed, despite Wilbur's efforts to place them in the tradition of righteous anger, as with the just quoted Miltonic sonnet. Take his "Speech for the Repeal of the McCarren Act" as another example. Wilbur invokes Mercian figures as the basis for his central metaphor, but his rhetorical impulses still get the better of his poetic ones. In short, the style of his utterance in this hectoring vein seems to be adapted, not natural. And I attribute this to temperament. Some poets can make poems out of spleen so that their poetry seems a logical extension of their talent. But Wilbur's poems in this genre seem muscled into being; they lose in similitude what they gain in directness, and poetry is in the former more than in the latter. I will rest my case by quoting a few lines as evidence from a poem Wilbur wrote in 1970 entitled "For the Student Strikers."

> Go talk with those who are rumored to be unlike you,
> And whom, it is said, you are so unlike.
> Stand on the stoops of their houses and tell them why
> You are out on strike.
>
> It is not yet time for the rock, the bullet, the blunt
> Slogan that fuddles the mind toward force.
> Let the new sound in our street be the patient sound
> Of your discourse.

Having expressed what is probably my only reservation about Wilbur's talent, I now feel free to praise. And I have no intention of being stingy in my praise of a man who, in poetic terms, is possibly the Mozart of our time. What Mozart achieved in music has a counterpart in Wilbur's achievement in poetry, particularly in his sense of symmetry, his uncanny precision of word choice, his almost infallible ear, his sense of humor as well as his sense of the tragic within a historical and literary tradition that he knows only too well, and, finally, his basic Christian ethos and the worldview that it nurtures.

To speak of Wilbur's sense of symmetry means more than the appearance of the poem on the page, although even from that perspective the basic layout of a Wilbur poem gives one an immediate impression of entirety—an impression that a subsequent reading of the poem immediately confirms. His poems end in conclusions, not confusions. The conclusions may flow from an idea advanced early in the poem, or, as in "Piazza de Spagna, Early Morning," the elaboration of a single image:

> I can't forget
> How she stood at the top of that long marble stair
> Amazed, and then with a sleepy pirouette
> Went dancing slowly down to the fountain-quieted square.
>
> Nothing upon her face
> But some impersonal loneliness,—not then a girl,
> But as it were a reverie of the place,
> A called-for failing glide and whirl;
>
> As when a leaf, petal, or thin chip
> Is drawn to the falls of a pool and circling a moment above
> it,
> Rides on over the lip—
> Perfectly beautiful, perfectly ignorant of it.

He does something quite similar in "A Glance from the Bridge."

> Letting the eyes descend from reeking stack
> And black façade to where the river goes,
> You see the freeze has started in to crack
> (As if the city squeezed it in a vise),
> And here and there the limbering water shows,
> And gulls colonial on the sullied ice.
>
> Some rise and braid their glidings white and spare,
> Or sweep the hemmed-in river up and down,
> Making a litheness in the barriered air,
> And through the town the freshening water swirls

As if an ancient whore undid her gown
And showed a body almost like a girl's.

The most regular poetic progressions in Wilbur's work appear in the riddle poems or what's-my-name poems that have been part of his writing from the very beginning (they spilled over delightfully into a book called *Opposites* whose meters challenge and whose rhymes please both children and adults.) These poems are not mere puzzles to be solved; they have about them a wit and whimsy that keeps them enjoyable even after the solution is known. The poetry is in their very structure and resolution with each poem ending, as Yeats once said of good poems in general, like the lid of a jewelry box being snapped shut. Here, for example, is one of the riddles of Symphosius describing coinage:

Another name I gained when I was fired;
I'm earth no more, but through me earth's acquired.

Another example of Wilbur's sense of symmetry, though somewhat atypical, is the following single image entitled "Sleepless at Crown Point":

All night, this headland
Lunges into the rumpling
Capework of the wind.

This symmetry in Wilbur's best poems is never imposed. It seems to proceed from the poetic seed out of which each poem grows, and Wilbur is artist enough (negatively capable enough, to use Keats' phrase) to go with the flow of this poetic energy until the poem has completed itself. If his poems were chairs or tables, I would always be convinced that their sutures and fastenings were secure and that they could stand on their own. At least, this has been my experience. I know from my reading of his work for more than forty years that he has never permitted himself to release something for publication that is not complete. At a time when some of his contemporaries regard opaqueness as a virtue rather than a sign of immaturity, this is no small triumph. And, of course, Wilbur's ongoing concern with the exact meaning and connotation and sound of words is a further aspect of his talent that places him in direct (and, for me, happy) opposition to some modern poets described as by C. M. Cioran in his *Anathemas and Admirations* as follows:

> Poetry is threatened when poets take too lively a theoretical interest in language and make it into a constant subject of meditation, when they confer upon it an exceptional status.... If we are truly to think, thought must adhere to the mind; if it becomes independent of the mind, exterior to it, the mind is shackled from the start, idles, and has but one source left—itself—instead of relying on the world for its substance or its pretexts. The writer must guard against reflecting obsessively upon language, must avoid making it the subject of his obsessions, must never forget that the important works have been created *despite* language. Dante was obsessed with what he had to say, not by the saying of it.

I do not think it presumptuous to claim that these words might have been written by Wilbur himself since his concern has always been with the things of this world and how to re-create them in language; in any case, I doubt if he would take exception to them. He is concerned with language the way that a landscape painter is concerned with paint. He constantly searches for the right word as a painter might search for the right (the exactly right) color to express his vision. He identifies the song of bells, for example, as the "the selfsame toothless voice for death or bridal." He alludes at just the right moment in "The Melongene" to the purple presence of an eggplant and, presto, we are in the eggplant's presence. In "Potato" he is able to distinguish the pure potato smell: "Cut open raw," in two lines: the essence of it "looses a cool clean stench,/ Mineral acid seeping from pores of priest meal." His poetic obituary to Phelps Putnam ("To an American Poet Just Dead") contains the "ssshh of sprays on all the little lakes" and an allusion to immortality as a "higher standard of living." In "Driftwood" he writes of "the great generality of waters" and the "warped" pieces having the look of "excellence earned" by retaining "their dense/ingenerate grain." In "An Event" he perceives in the zigzag of clouds of birds in flight "By what cross-purposes the world is dreamt." And "A Baroque Wall-Fountain in the Villa Sciara" contains one of the best re-creations of the sound and sight of fountaining water that I have ever encountered in any literature:

> Happy in all that ragged, loose
> Collapse of water, its effortless descent
>
> And flatteries of spray,
> The stocky god upholds the shell with ease,
> Watching, about his craggy knees,
> The goatish innocence of his babes at play;
>
> His fauness all the while
> Leans forward, slightly, into the clambering mesh
> Of water-lights, her sparkling flesh
> In a saecular ecstasy, her blinded smile
>
> Bent on the sand floor
> Of the trefoil pool, where ripple-shadows come
> And go in swift reticulum,
> More addling to the eye than wine, and more

Interminable to thought
Than pleasure's calculus. Yet since this all
Is pleasure, flash, and waterfall,
Must it not be too simple? Are we not

More intricately expressed
In the plain fountains that Maderna set
Before St. Peter's—the main jet
Struggling aloft until it seems to rest

In the very act of rising, until
The very wish of water is reversed,
That heaviness borne up to burst
In a clear high, cavorting head, to fill

With blaze, and then in gauze
Delays, in a gnatlike shimmering, in a fine
Illumined version of itself, decline
And patter on the stones its own applause.

It is in stanzas like these that one can detect how Wilbur's ear rarely fails him. The matching of sound and rhythm to the rise and fall of fountaining water is so unobtrusively true that we actually hear as well as see the "wish of water" in and through the language. I for one admire the subtlety here of Wilbur's musical sense more than I do some of the onomatopoetic stanzas of "On Freedom's Ground" (Part IV) where he attempts to replicate the rhythms of waltzes, polkas, cakewalks, and jigs. Of course, these replications occur in a cantata where the words cannot be divorced from the musical background—they are lyrics, after all—, but I find the silent music of the lines he wrote to evoke the waterflow of the Villa Sciara fountain more poetic.

As he has grown older, Wilbur has not abandoned the formal hallmarks of his earlier style (as Karl Shapiro did, for example) but adapted them to different subjects with the same jeweler's eye and musician's ear for the right world in the right place at exactly the right time. Poems like "The Fire-Truck" and "The Undead" from *Advice to a Prophet* (1961) testify to this as does the book's powerful title poem. Nor does Wilbur's basic style change in *Walking to Sleep* (1969) in such poems as "For Dudley," "Playboy," and "A Late Aubade."

The poem called "Shame" in *Advice to a Prophet* is a happy aberration. True, the lines are basically iambic pentameter lines, but they are certainly not in the tradition of Pope's precise ten-syllabled pentameters. Wilbur hews to five feet per line, but he plays fast and loose with the syllabic count, and the poem is much better for it because the fastness and looseness match the theme. This is one of the few poems in which Wilbur just lets himself go, and his sense of mild sarcasm, his basic good humor and his almost Rabelaisian swagger here and there (usually hidden elsewhere to the point of invisibility) rise and flourish to the plain delight of any fair-minded reader. Anyone familiar with the poem knows how the unspecified country of "Shame" achieves its ultimate victory over its conquerors and occupiers. Wilbur informs us early in the poem that this is a nation with "no foreign policy," an unfathomable grammar, a national sense of its own unimportance, and a geography "best described as unrelieved." The people's chief weapon seems to be self-deprecation wedded to self-disdain. Left alone, they turn these weapons on themselves and manage thus to perpetuate their own mediocrity and undisguised mendacity. After all, this is a country whose "national product" is sheep and whose people truly believe that "they do not count" and who confirm this by announcing that the population total is "zero."

Yet, their very vices make them invincible when they confront the "hoped-for invasion" with "complete negligence" and "overwhelming submission." The result is that they conquer their conquerors by slowly imbuing them with their own vices:

Their complete negligence is reserved, however,
For the hoped-for invasion, at which time the happy people
(Sniggering, ruddily naked, and shamelessly drunk)
Will stun the foe by their overwhelming submission,
Corrupt the generals, infiltrate the staff,
Usurp the throne, proclaim themselves to be sun-gods
And bring about the collapse of the whole empire.

Further confirming Wilbur's sense of artistic restraint during the sixties are two touchstone poems—one from *Advice to a Prophet* and the other from *Walking to Sleep.* The title poem from *Advice to a Prophet* is not a direct but a slantwise comment on the possibility of a nuclear apocalypse, though Wilbur eschews the apocalyptic tone and pose so readily assumed by numerous other poets dealing with the same subject. He asks not to be informed about "the weapons, their force and range," nor does he want to be told for the zillionth time about the possible extinction of humanity ("Nor shall you scare us with talk of the death of the race"). Instead, Wilbur considers the realizable desolation we would immediately know if certain specific animals or birds were to disappear from the earth as we know it. He does not speak in general or abstract terms of the death of mankind but of finite, definite absences, and the sense of loss that is at the heart of the poem grows out of these anticipated absences:

...Though we cannot conceive
Of an undreamt thing, we know to our cost
How the dreamt cloud crumbles, the vines are blackened
  by frost,
How the view alters. We could believe

If you told us so, that the white-tailed deer will slip
Into perfect shade, grown perfectly shy,

The lark avoid the reaches of our eye,
The jack-pine lose its knuckled grip

On the cold ledge, and every torrent burn
As Xanthus, once, its gliding trout
Stunned in a twinkling. What should we be without
The dolphin's arc, the dove's return

These things in which we have seen ourselves and spoken?
Ask us, prophet, how we shall call
Our natures forth when that live tongue is all
Dispelled, that glass obscured or broken

In which we have said the rose of our love and the clean
Horse of our courage, in which beheld
The singing locust of the soul unshelled,
And all we mean, or wish to mean.

The power of this poem derives from how we respond to those prophesied and enumerated losses and the effect their absence will have on how we define our very lives. The extent of this loss is left to our imaginations. In terror as in art, less proves to be more, much more.

The poem "Running" from *Walking to Sleep* is structurally a typical Wilbur poem—a series of introductory descriptions in each section with each ambience counterbalanced by the poet's reaction to it. All three sections deal straightforwardly with the joyful exhilaration of running or of observing runners in action. In the first section Wilbur remembers running in Caldwell, New Jersey, in 1933. The lickety-split run becomes an absolute in his memory when he writes—"Thinking of happiness, I think of that." Skipping the second section for a moment, we find in the third section a self-description where Wilbur, running as an older man, comes upon two boys running in the opposite direction. As they prepare to pass one another, they rhyme for a moment simply as runners, and Wilbur senses the exhilaration of youth from that passing moment. But it is in the second section that we find the correlative that is possibly an inadvertent profile that Wilbur gives of himself. Wilbur, now a non-participant, focuses on one of the runners in a race:

> Dark in the glare, they seemed to thresh in place
> Like preening flies upon a window-sill,
> Yet gained and grew, and at a cruel pace
> Swept by us on their way to Heartbreak Hill—
>
> Legs driving, fists at port, clenched faces, men,
> And in amongst them, stamping on the sun,
> Our champion Kelley, who would win again,
> Rocked in his will, at rest within his run.

The style of Kelley's run is a perfect match for Wilbur's style as a writer—a man sure of his skills and strengths, secure within his own skin, husbanding his known resources and then pitting them against nothing but the challenge before him, confident that he is equal to it.

It may not be important to some to identify humor as one of Wilbur's poetic assets, but I for one believe it is. Humor is also a sign of a person with a sense of spiritual balance. Although Robert Lowell was and remains a poet of genuine stature and has been identified as a more cosmic poet than Wilbur, one must look long and hard to find a Lowell poem with a smile on its face. Nonetheless, a sense of humor would have gone a long way to acquaint us with his very humanity and not merely with his personal demons. Wilbur's humor, whether ribald enough to provoke a loud guffaw or subtle enough to coax a good chuckle, is never mean-spirited or silly. Its aim seems to be pure fun whether it has a satirical edge or not. And this is true of his earlier poems ("Superiorities," "Parable," "Museum Piece") as well as of subsequent ones ("Shame,"

"Matthew VIII, 28ff.," "A Late Aubade," "The Prisoner of Zenda," "To His Skeleton"). The spirit of humor in "Matthew VII, 28ff." is a typical example:

> Rabbi, we Gadarenes
> Are not ascetics; we are fond of wealth and possessions.
> Love, as you call it, we obviate by means
> Of the planned release of aggressions.
>
> We have deep faith in prosperity.
> Soon, it is hoped, we will reach our full potential.
> In the light of the gross product, the practice of charity
> Is palpably inessential.
>
> It is true that we go insane;
> That for no good reason we are possessed by devils;
> That we suffer, despite the amenities which obtain
> At all but the lowest levels.
>
> We shall not, however, resign
> Our trust in the high-heaped table and the full trough.
> If you cannot cure us without destroying our swine,
> We had rather you shoved off.

The barely concealed criticism of the smugly rich in this poem somehow does not get in the way of the roistering, and by the time we get to the last line we are smiling our way into a good laugh.

To move from Wilbur's humorous poems to such masterpieces as "Love Calls Us to the Thing of This World," "The Writer," "Cottage Street, 1953," and a love poem to his wife Charlee ("For C") in *Mayflies* is to realize that Wilbur is not a man who, like some of the confessionalists of his generation, eschews the lightsome in order to be properly glum. Not at all. His is a sensibility which permits him to respond to and re-create in his poetry the light as well as the weighty, the smile as well as the frown. And who can deny that a complete vision of human life does not, after all, include them both?

Now to a consideration of the ethos of Wilbur's talent. That Wilbur has a theocentric view of life is traceable not only to those poems of his that have liturgical or theological themes, i.e., "A Christmas Hymn," "A Wedding Toast," "For Dudley," "John Chrysostom," to name but a few of the many, but to a deeper and unmistakable spirituality that infuses his entire corpus and is unfeignable. Three poems from his total oeuvre reveal to me the three salient aspects of his spirituality. The first is a crypto-poem called "The Proof" that is both a prayer and, in its succinctness, a further variation of the telegrammic style found in his riddles. The second is "Love Calls Us to the Things of This World," a poem which, in its acceptance of the given world and its transfiguration in words, is as consummate a realization as I know of what the calling of a poet as a seer really means. And the third is "Cottage Street, 1952," because of all that stands behind the naked judgment of the final line.

The tone of "The Proof" (with tone defined as the author's attitude toward his subject, his audience and himself) is as revealing of Wilbur's sensibility as is the very subject of the poem. From the first word to the last the author reveals himself as a trusting and humble man who is willing to abandon himself to the mercy and generosity of God. It is as if Wilbur has taken the biblical injunction that fear of the Lord is the beginning of wisdom and made it the very soul of the poem. I have detected this same tone in numerous other poems of his (and in some of his translations as well). It is never forced nor fictitious. Somehow one is able to sense when one is the presence of genuine feelings of this nature, and the feelings aroused by "The Proof" impress me in this way.

> Shall I love God for causing me to be?
> I was mere utterance; shall these words love me?

Yet when I caused his work to jar and stammer,
And one free subject loosened all his grammar,

I love him that he did not in a rage
Once and forever rule me off the page

But, thinking I might come to please him yet,
Crossed out *delete* and wrote his patient *stet*.

This poem has the unmistakable resignation and deference of personal prayer. It is this deference that appears again and again in Wilbur's poetry—a deference to things as they are in their God-created or man-created uniqueness, a deference to the beautiful and its changes, a deference to love itself and a willingness to allow it the space it needs to manifest itself and grow.

Perhaps no poem in all of Wilbur's writings affirms his wonder in the presence of God-created or man-created things than his much and deservedly anthologized "Love Calls Us to the Things of This World." Rather than quote the poem in its entirety since it is one of Wilbur's best known works, I will allude only to the basic circumstance of the poem and how Wilbur, presumably the persona of the poem, finds in that circumstance a reason to affirm and bless it.

A sleeper is slowly coming awake. He imagines that the laundry hanging on the clothesline outside his window is a flight of seraphim. This angelic laundry seems to float and dance in the "false dawn" of semi-wakefulness:

Now they are rising together in calm swells
Of halcyon feeling, filling whatever they were
With the deep joy of their impersonal breathing

But such a Platonic view has only a limited lease on the observer's life, and, despite how he wants the illusion to persist in defiance of the upcoming "punctual rape of every blessed day," he knows that the soul must descend "once more in bitter love/To accept the waking body." And, of course, since form and function are destined to exist in consonance, the hanging laundry, which exists finally to be worn, must come down from its "ruddy gallows." It must clothe thieves, lovers and nuns; the world must go on being the world. The pivotal image of the lovers ("Let lovers go fresh and sweet to be undone") provides the ironic balance between the thieves and the nuns, since lovers go dressed only to the point when they must undo their clothes so that they can become lovers in fact—lovemakers. Regardless of the irony, the entire poem ends on the side of life and "the things of this world" where only love can humanize us, not in otherworldly but in this-worldly terms. Like Frost, Wilbur assumes that "earth's the right place for love." Thus, the waking body offsets the bitterness of its dream-ending moment of false bliss by quite literally blessing (what is an affirmation, after all, but a blessing?) the real world where theft, loving and devotion are ongoing and co-existent.

"Cottage Street, 1953" is Wilbur at his lyrical and perspicacious best. The setting could not be more plain—a tea on Cottage Street hosted by Edna Ward, Wilbur's mother-in-law. Present are Wilbur himself, his wife, a young Sylvia Plath and her mother. Wilbur admits to having been invited so as to serve as a role model for the despondent Sylvia.

> It is my office to exemplify
> The published poet in his happiness,
> Thus cheering Sylvia, who has wished to die;
> But half-ashamed, and impotent to bless,
>
> I am a stupid life-guard who has found
> Swept to his shallows by the tide, a girl

Who, far from shore, has been immensely drowned
And stares through water now with eyes of pearl.

The ongoing "refusal" of Sylvia Plath to do anything but drown is in sharp contrast with the quiet courage of Edna Ward, destined to die a decade and a half later (the poem was obviously written after 1968) but doing so with tearless dignity and speaking of love to and at the very end. Against the example of Edna Ward's graced and graceful death at the age of eighty-eight, Wilbur describes Sylvia Plath as one who in her despair seemed "condemned to live" and whose poetry's "brilliant negative" seemed on balance "free and helpless and unjust." It is the mention of injustice that tells us how Wilbur perceives the lives of these two radically different women—the elder, who is a valiant example of keeping faith with life even in extremis, and the younger, who is a victim not so much of life as of her twisted vision of it. Weighing Edna Ward's bravery against the spiritual self-betrayal of Sylvia Plath who, at the time of the writing of this poem, had already taken her own life, Wilbur comes down on the side of justice—justice to life itself. This transmutes the poem into a double elegy, and, as elegies tell us more about life when touched with death than they tell us about life itself (since death is actually unknowable), they reveal the human values of the elegist himself. Ultimately Wilbur pities Sylvia Plath; he is edified by Edna Ward.

This brings me full circle in my estimate of Richard Wilbur. (I should add that Wilbur is an equally talented reader of his own poems and translations. Whoever has listened to him before an audience has experienced what Wilbur himself ascribed once to the work of Degas —"Beauty joined to energy.") My few reservations, which I felt obliged to include in the spirit of absolute candor, are but quibbles in the balance. Far exceeding them is the wealth of poems that will be part of our literature as long as it lasts. For that we can only be quick to praise and, above all, be grateful.

At Odds with the Overdone

Suppose you saw in bold print where it could not be missed—"Sickle Cell Anemia's the Great White Hope." Or "Send a Cuban Home for Christmas." Or "Arabs Can Go and Reproduce Themselves." I saw all three of these statements at three different times. They were printed on white T-shirts worn by three different men. Or suppose you saw at a formal dinner a pregnant woman in a full-length black evening dress with the word "L'Infante" woven in white on the front of the dress just below her neck. Beneath "L'Infante" was a white arrow pointing southward to her abdomen.

I cite these examples not only as examples of malice or bad taste but because they represent a new dimension in what is known as publication. Publication these days is quite simple and answerable only to the publisher, who is often just one person. That person can say whatever he or she wishes on T-shirts ("Beauty Is in the Eye of the Beer Holder"), bumper stickers ("I Do What I Want"), matchbook covers ("Experience Celery") or an evening dress. Throw in internet websites, and you have what bona-fide publishing or even desk-top publishing have as their ever-widening competition. And, of course, I have not even alluded to graffiti. In city after city spray painters can leave their messages on walls or whatever and be assured that they will be read by passersby. In some cases, their handiwork has even been applauded as outdoor art instead of being excoriated as the vandalism it actually is.

As eye-catching as some of these outbursts may be, they all share one thing in common. They appear on surfaces (fabric, car bumpers, computer screens and anything that will absorb spray paint). They have the one dimension that only surfaces can give—a brief flatness. They are to public discourse what the smart quip is to mere gossip or what the soundbite is to narration on television—startling, seemingly incisive or even shocking at the moment but with no follow-up. What insights can be gained or what conclusions drawn from the presence in society of people who have the need to express themselves in such ways? What does it say of society itself where such habits of mind are spawned and where such spawnings seem to be multiplying? The examples I have noted are curious, to say the least, but are they in fact the psychotic, neurotic or simply bizarre sideshows of what our mainstreaming impatience with deeper thinking has made possible?

Is it over-generalizing to suggest that we may have grown into a society not particularly sensitive to subtlety or nuance, particularly in public matters? Because we prefer our daily realities to be as clear as headlines, it seems we are impatient with what is not immediately obvious. We tend to overlook the fine points of many things in favor of what is blatantly apparent, whether the apparent is significant or not. We assume that the apparent and the real are synonymous even though we know from experience and from both literature and philosophy that appearances are frequently deceiving and even at odds with reality in instance after instance. Invariably we forget that truth lies in details and that these details often elude first sight. Or even second sight. The mischief created by this misperception has generated an urgency, especially among the more impressionable young and the perpetually immature, to think that significance is directly proportionate to notice.

According to this philosophy—to make your mark, be noticeable. To be noticeable, be obvious. And if obviousness fails, be ostentatious. In other words, show off. Originally this dictated a difference in dress, in language, in social habits, in politics and in taste across the board. In the fifties and sixties, for example, the cult of the obvious was personified by the so-called Beat Generation. In a poem called "Howl" the most prominent poet of that generation, Allen Ginsberg, wrote: "I saw the best minds of my generation destroyed by madness—starving, hysterical, naked." Who, apart from Ginsberg and those who shared his vision, said that these were the best minds of that generation? Who said so then, and who says so now? Yet this piece of self-serving braggadocio became a landmark for literary and cultural critics of American poetry at mid-century. Many journalists and social historians swallowed it whole and claimed, with some but certainly not total justification, that the Beats brought poetry out of the closet and into the coffee shop. True, the Beats did much to restore poetry as an oral or bardic art, but Dylan Thomas certainly did more and with much greater artistry. Still, obviousness took precedence over a truly consummate talent, and Thomas receives much less credit than he deserves for making a poet-at-the-platform the proper position for poets after mid-century.

Woodstock (the first Woodstock and not its recent progeny that ended in similar and even more serious mischief) generated another myth, and social commentators had a field day drawing conclusions about the American character because of the behavior of the attendees, as if anyone who was not at Woodstock was either wrongheaded or asleep. A cult grew up around it and around those who performed there. Careers were generated, books written, social standards set. All of this strikes me as a classical example of mere notoriety (plus, to be fair, some talent) transformed into genuine fame. But ostentation and marketing had a lot to do with it, as did the growing resistance of many of the young to the tragedy known as the Vietnam War. The fact remains that Woodstockian behavior was not the only form of resistance to that war; there were others, many others, but they were simply not as obvious. Because they were not obvious, it was assumed by many at the time that they simply did not exist.

As the sixties and seventies progressed, the cult of the deliberately ugly began to assert itself. This in turn created the reactionary counterforce of the so-called politically correct and in turn the "Religious Right," who err on the side of rigidity and righteousness respectively. Both the ugly and the fanatically correct confuse appearances with essences until their positions on almost anything became and remain boringly predictable. To call them merely reactionary is only half a description. The obviousness of their position is often directly proportionate to what their opponents flaunt. And this means that we have a classic case of obviousness answering obviousness in the most obvious way possible. The current manifestation of tribal obviousness is the tattoo as well as the sporting of metal on or in the skin—rings embedded in the eyebrows, lips, tongue, ears (lobes and otherwise), nostrils and elsewhere south of the chin and even south of the navel. Tattoos, of course, have a history among primitives as did body-painting among the Native Americans. They tattooed or painted themselves to show they were different from animals. Today there seems to be no such motivation beyond showing-off at best and peer pressure at worst. Semanticists might claim that such decorations are themselves a form of free speech, and, semantically speaking, they are correct. But what the unsaid words (the hidden details) of this language of decoration say is nothing more or less than: "Notice me, notice how I've transformed myself. Love me, love my tattoos and body-rings." In short, this is just personal advertisement, and it owes a lot to marketing. Many have blamed the media for publicizing and popularizing the eccentric by giving it notice. This, of course, can no more be attributed to the media than vehicular accidents can be made totally the fault of automobiles. Any medium is just what it implies—a halfway link between subject and object. If this is true, then what is focused on often says more about the focuser than what he has in his sights. If media directors focus on the bizarre or the catastrophic (as they admittedly do), the decisions to do so lie with those who are doing the focusing. If it is a human inclination to be attracted to the bizarre simply because it is different, the focusers will concentrate on the bizarre in the same way and for the same reason that they concentrate on the catastrophic, the violent or the prurient. There is a public appetite for these subjects, and this appetite is insatiable. Buoyed by demand and sales, the media simply feeds this appetite, and the cycle goes on perpetuating itself. Catastrophe becomes entertainment, prurience and gossip qualify as human interest, and mere celebrity (people who are famous for no other reason than that they are famous) creates a separate social class whose real value is inversely proportionate to real worth.

It stands to reason that the cultural trend that is created by ostentation is bound to have its imitators and exploiters. The only person in my memory who used ostentation but was not used by it was Muhammed Ali. He was intelligent enough to use the tricks of notice to draw attention to himself and his career goals, but he never became a servant of his own tactics. Indeed, he often made fun of them and even of himself in public to show who the boss really was. But most others, like the high-fiving and jackassing characters who disport in the endzone after a touchdown, do not have the talent or the character to disabuse themselves of their own exhibitionism. It would be incorrect to assume that ostentation is always equatable with noise and overkill. The technicians of ostentation, particularly in the field of advertising, have transformed their techniques into an art form. And it seems not farfetched to note that advertising, despite its subliminal appeals to pride, vanity, power and other impulses, is also a surface art, whether the surface be a billboard, a page, a screen image or a vocal "pitch" with musical enhancement. The basic formula is that what gains notice is adoptable; what does not, isn't. Consequently, there are numerous examples of calculated understatement employed as a way of attracting attention, and they invariably succeed. Perhaps this is because the public, surfeited with overloaded ads and promotional pieces, is simply relieved by the contrast. The motion picture industry, although not known for understatement, will occasionally use this to good effect. The careful promotion of Stanley Kubrick's *Eyes Wide Shut* is the most recent example. No advance stills or footage were ever permitted in the promotion. It seems to have been decided that the names of Kubrick, Tom Cruise and Nicole Kidman were sufficient, and teaser ads appeared here and there like lighted fuses that would eventually lead to the big explosion. In this connection it is interesting to note that advertising to the motion picture industry is an absolutely indispensable ally. Although advertising is crucial to the prosperity of most industries, it occupies a unique position of importance for Hollywood. The reason is, as the descendant of one of the original movie moguls expressed it, that movies are one of the only industries where people pay before they know what they are getting. Advertising serves the vital purpose of inveigling people to purchase a ticket; its mission is to guarantee attendance, not satisfaction. With this in mind the advertising technicians employ a chromatic scale of approaches from the aforementioned understatement to forms of overstatement that give hyperbole a bad name.

Because many people are inclined to equate importance with public notice, and because public notice is often gained through publicity, it seems inevitable that there are some in any society who will seek publicity—by whatever means—as a way of being considered important or, at least, significant. What else can explain the behavior of Dennis Rodman on or off the basketball court? And what has been the purpose of the boorishness and outright effrontery of comedians like Groucho Marx and Don Rickles except to gain publicity and notice? And, in each of these cases, it seems to have worked. I suppose the same logic would apply to those who commit crimes as a way to secure their moment in the sun. One of the most recent examples is the murderous spree by two adolescents at Columbine High School in Colorado. Another would be the modus operandi of the Unabomber, swapping his threats of further bombings for the opportunity to have his capitalist anti-manifestoes published for the world to see. And one cannot forget that the assassinations or attempted assassinations of our Presidents from Lincoln onward, with the curious exception of the murder of President Kennedy, have been committed by men who, by claiming so or by allowing themselves no means of escape, wanted to be known as the perpetrators. In all of these cases the end was seen as justifying the means. If the means involved murder by gun or letter-bomb, the end of gaining fifteen-minutes of fame was seen as being well worth it. A person could be transformed from invisibility to world-wide visibility in a matter of a single day, and his name would be forever linked with infamy mistaken for fame.

Earlier, I mentioned that notoriety and fame tend to be considered as synonymous even though they are by nature different. Notoriety can easily be defined as recognition gained by any means possible. In this sense John Wilkes Booth, Gorgeous George and the "streaker" who interrupted the Academy Awards ceremony almost a decade ago can be described as notorious. Notoriety is thus something that is actively sought by word or action. Fame, on the contrary, is something that is bestowed. In this sense it is like happiness. Happiness rarely accommodates those who assiduously seek it. Rather it is a gift that comes to someone as the result of a particular action done for its own sake at a particular time with no hope or thought of reward. Fame answers to the same criterion. Thomas Jefferson's writing of the Declaration of Independence, Rosa Parks' refusal to move to the "back of the bus," Pope John XXIII's supposedly spontaneous decision to convene the Vatican Council and the countless Congressional Medal of Honor awardees who lost their lives while attempting to save others are people genuinely deserving of being called famous, although all would probably have been embarrassed by the designation.

Notoriety is in some ways related to publicity, regardless of the nature of that publicity. In business the dictum exists that bad publicity is better than no publicity at all. Even bad publicity has the virtue of keeping the name of the business in front of the public, which means no more than stating that publicity of any kind is better than neglect. In many circles publicity often is interpreted as a sign of business growth. Since one of the fundamental principles of commerce is that a business is either growing or it is dying, this dependence on publicity for continued economic life is not a negligible matter. Because growth in this sense means getting bigger (if not better), it's only a hop, skip and jump to see how easily publicity could transform itself into ostentation, all for the sake of ongoing name recognition and an enhanced image of "bigness."

The long-term effects of ostentation are all too apparent, but they do nothing to discourage the continuation of the trend. This tendency is so ingrained in our culture that it often continues in the lives of those whose careers when young owed much to publicity per se. Nothing, for example, is more pathetic than to see self-deluded people, i.e. movie stars who are over the hill, some athletes who are past their prime, politicians who try to make a comeback, veterans who are always preparing for the last war, re-appear in public and try their damnedest to be who they used to be when the evidence indicates otherwise. To say this about them is to risk becoming identified as a mere scold or spoilsport, but it only shows how those once habituated to the notoriety of mere recognition find it difficult to do without it.

Ostentatious phenomena, whether it be the spin-offs created by the O. J. Simpson case, the Gulf War parades (no war disappeared from public memory faster than that), the Academy Awards hoopla (the spectacle of an industry applauding itself in public) or the dalliances between Dr. Lewinsky's daughter and the President of the United States, do not have a long shelf-life. They can't hold a candle in the long run to the often-overlooked qualities of modesty, candor, talent, patience and genuine stature. Such qualities shy away from marketing themselves, as their very natures would indicate. But they have the one asset that ostentation lacks. They endure. Above all, they endure on their own terms.

One Myth Too Many

"Whoever said that athletes or any other public figures had to be role models?" a friend of mine asked me recently. Then he added, "My role model was my father." This immediately made me realize that many people may be looking for role models in the wrong places and for the wrong reasons. The reasons for this misdirection may be rooted in myths. Sports has its ongoing myths from Frank Merriwell to the Gipper, and these myths often transfer to baseball and football players across the board. The assumption is that athletic prowess and moral probity and civility are necessarily synonymous. Pete Rose is the most obvious exception to the rule, but there are others. In the realm of politics, the myths of George Washington and the cherry tree plus the later one of Honest Abe prod us to see idealism in public figures where none exists. If sanctity is the chief prerequisite for those holding public office, as the myth suggests, the House of Representatives and the Senate would be practically vacant.

Apart from sports and politics, to what extent do myths exert their influences? Everybody remembers, for example, how Snow White was bewitched into ongoing sleep until she was awakened by a prince's kiss. Is there some connection between this fairy tale and how in fact some women (as well as some men) can be awakened from a soporific and deadening life by the sudden kiss of love in their lives? And what about the myth of Pinocchio, the wooden puppet who was finally loved into life? Is this not similar to our habit of humanizing things or pets because we have a special partiality or even an affection for them? In fact, don't we see this constantly and openly in children who have special dolls or toys (think of Linus' blanket as a case in point) that assume a life of their own because the children love them? Something of the myth of Pinocchio is common to all these examples.

Fairy tales and myths have been defined as stories that are partly true and partly not. Snow White is obviously not a true story, but the implications of the story are true without a doubt. The implications have a counterpart in the lives we live, and this often explains how myths (not just post-facto but a priori) exert a compelling influence on our outlook and behavior—frequently a more compelling influence than we ascribe to human reason. The ancient Egyptians, for example, believed that the phoenix (part dream, part actual flamingo or ibis) rose anew from its own ashes, and the myth of the phoenix has remained a symbol of death and resurrection to this very day. Then there is the seductress Circe in Homer's *Odyssey* who beguiled and surfeited the crew of Odysseus so that they were transformed into pigs, which is as good a symbol for human carnality as anyone might imagine. And later in the same story Homer describes a country of one-eyed people, and we see an immediate connection between these people and the hopelessly narrow-minded and tunnel-visioned. And in Greek and Egyptian mythology we have the figures of the satyr (human headed with the lower body of a goat) and the sphynx (human headed with the torso of a lion), and we cannot help but concluded that this is how the Greeks and the Egyptians envisioned two dominant aspects of man's nature—man as a lecher and man as a predator. And in our own time myths continue to proliferate and influence the lives of those who are affected, however subliminally, by them —"Blondes have more fun"—"Real men don't cry"—"Diamonds are a girl's best friend"—"Those who can, do; those who can't, teach." The list is infinite.

Considering the range of myths in modern life, the three that seem to predominate are those involving money, appearances and knowledge. All the monetary myths originate in the perception of money not as a medium of exchange, which is its essence, but as something with its own dynamic worth. Often this perceived worth is equated with human worth, as reflected in the saying, "How much is he or she worth?" Money is also associated with fecundity, i.e., money makes money (except for those whose investments come up dry). It also carries over to speech, i.e., money *talks* (as if those without money have no right to be heard). And, of course, it has implications in domestic life, i.e., money marries money (a perfect definition of a merge rather than a marriage).

The myth of appearances actually has come to mean false appearances. The image industries are built on this premise, and fortunes are spent on creating the right image, which is nothing more than how the image-makers want their subject to be perceived. Nixon became "the new Nixon," for example, as if anyone's personal identity can be changed overnight. Cosmetic surgeons (as distinguished from reconstructive surgeons) are called upon regularly to change the way people were born to look. All of this legerdemain is based upon the principle that "Perception equals reality," and this in turn presumes that people are unable to distinguish between appearance and essence, which in turn assumes that people can be easily duped. In a word, suckers.

Perhaps the most egregious myth of all these days is the one involving knowledge. It is assumed by many that someone who "knows a lot" is automatically more intelligent than those who do not. This is buttressed by the availability to one and all of "the information highway" on the internet, by quiz shows, by the belief that information and real knowledge are one and the same. People are transformed into watchers rather than readers as the screen gradually replaces the page. As a result, information-zealots are quite high on having computers accessible to the young from childhood on since they believe that the well informed will automatically evolve into an intelligent citizenry. The fact is that this is not automatic at all. There are legions of well informed, stupid people. Not ignorant but stupid. They make bad judgments. They have pathetic taste. They don't know the difference between what is worth knowing and what is negligible. Their so-called knowledge never gets beyond the information stage. It is never humanized. It never matures into wisdom, and wisdom after all is the one quality we expect the intelligent to possess. Being a winner on Jeopardy is not a sign of intelligence. Making the right decision at the right time is.

The myth of *Faust* by Goethe is the story of a man who wanted to know everything. The devil granted him this, but he lost his soul in the bargain. Many moderns are making Faust's mistake. They spend hours in front of "time-saving" computers and often have no time for themselves, which is tantamount to losing touch with yourself, which in turn means losing your soul. What does it profit anyone if he knows everything (which in itself is impossible) if he loses himself in the process? But the myth persists. Faust lives.

Brave New Century

For those who think the world began when they were born, history is often regarded as irrelevant. Drugged by news reports every hour on the hour by the hour, they are focused almost exclusively on the present tense. History is seen as nothing more than chronology like a calendar whose passing days are X-ed off as they pass. To suggest to them that the present is the future that the past made possible is usually a wasted effort.

Historically speaking, the United States has been engaged since year one of the present century in preparing for or waging a war in Iraq. The reason given was that Iraq was considered complicit in the 9/11 attacks. Many, including the instigators, knew this to be untrue, but the attack went ahead anyway. Baghdad fell. Curiously, the Oil Ministry was the only government institution that was protected under guard. Other institutions and priceless antiquities were left to vandals. Recently, Lord Tony Blair has admitted penitently that the pretext ("We are forty-five minutes away from being attacked...") for the war was fabricated, but, as a cover-up, he added the world was better off without Saddam Hussein. One could not help but wonder, even if one took Blair at his obsequious word, why more than 1,000,000 Iraqis had to be killed, many others sickened and wounded while 2,000,000 plus had to be driven from their homes in the process of sociocide. The oil wealth of Iraq and the pressure of Israeli interests were never mentioned in the mainstream media as influential.

To lead a country into war under false pretenses is by any standard the most heinous of treasons, but Bush, Cheney, Rumsfeld, Wolfowitz, Perle, the aforementioned Blair and the entire neo-con cabal remain audibly at large, writing op. eds. in major newspapers and still in positions of influence. In some quarters they are even held in high regard.

How much of the history of the previous century can be accessed to explain our behavior so far in the current one? The twentieth century began with the United States still savoring victory as a result of its self-aggrandizing war with Spain vis-à-vis Cuba and the Philippines. A decade and a half later we were involved in World War I. At its conclusion we had lost 116,516 Americans. In the then new age of total war that figure was considered small compared to the total death count on all sides of 11,000,000 military and 7,000,000 civilian deaths. In more personal terms it meant that the husbands, sons and husbands-to-be of 4,000,000 French and German women never came home. Later the punitive Treaty of Versailles and America's post-war isolationism assured the coming of another war, and the war came. When it ended, the sum of all deaths from World Wars I and II was 67,000,000. This is millions more than the entire current population of France, two times the population of Canada and more than 65 times the population of metropolitan Pittsburgh. One of the consequences of all this is that we have now become gradually inured to and less shocked by war deaths and casualties that number in the millions.

Then came a series of wars ("police actions," "surges" etc.) created by the divine right of presidents: Korea (36,516 Americans killed), Vietnam (58,229), Beirut (256), Afghanistan to date (2,356) and Iraq to date (4,489). And there were other interventions in El Salvador, Grenada, Panama and Somalia. We accepted Johnson's Pedernales statesmanship, "I don't want to spit in Ho Chi Minh's eye, and I don't want him to spit in mine." Under Reagan the Marine battalion that was stationed south of Beirut as "peacekeepers" were ordered to have no bullets in the chambers of their weapons. This explains why the guards could not stop a suicidal driver of a bomb-laden truck that rammed the building where the Marines were quartered. The deaths of 256 Marines remain the largest single-incident one-day loss of life in Marine Corps history after Iwo Jima.

What conclusions can be drawn from this albeit foreshortened historical survey? The first is that we have killed millions of people in Vietnam, the Middle East and elsewhere with impunity. The second is that we have come to accept war as an ongoing fact of life. Forget for the moment, if you can, the nuclear option, torture, government surveillance, war profiteering, murder by drone and the rest. War comes down to strangers killing or being killed by strangers. If we listen to the chicken hawks and war mongers, who believe we should fight the ultimate war of civilization against suicidal enemies now in Asia Minor, we should expect total mobilization, the possible revival of the draft as well as surveillance enhancement. We would be on a total war footing.

There is a dangerous hubris at work here—a militaristic belief that armed might makes all the difference—that might makes right. We have seen the tragic consequences of this in Korea, Vietnam and Iraq. All you have to do is listen to "deciders" like Lindsey Graham, Ted Cruz, Marco Rubio, Donald Trump, the unsinkable Sarah Palin and the viscerally hawkish Hillary Rodham Clinton to envision what kind of political leadership we might be awarded with to deal with this problem. They are the current version of those chicken hawks who claimed that the conquest of Iraq would be a cakewalk when General Eric Shinseki said it would take hundreds of thousands of troops to occupy Iraq. In fact, our foreign policies in the Middle East have in more ways than one created the very enemies we are now facing. The ongoing denial of sovereignty to the Palestinians remains *the* inflammatory issue throughout the Arab world, particularly as Israeli settlements illegally fracture the West Bank into little Gazas. And then there was the dismissal of the Iraqi army and government staffers by Paul Bremer that literally created ISIS. Nor can we ignore the destruction of Libya that forced the flight of thousands of Libyans to Europe via the Mediterranean but left in its place nothing but chaos and armed groups prepared to fight those who created it.

There is no question that we have the military and manufacturing capacity to deal with whatever may come, but where are the visionary leaders who understand a suicidal enemy? They are not among those for whom force is the first and only option. They are not the sloganeers who rarely think when they speak but simply pronounce. Candidates from both parties have honed this into a quasi-art with nothing behind it but more of the same. And unfortunately, the cakewalking chicken hawks are still there with their self-serving optimism. The prospects of vision at the highest level of government are poor at best. A Welsh lieutenant named Wilfred Owen, who was killed in the last week of World War I, wrote prophetically of what could be our lot. He wrote of war and "the pity of war" as one who experienced it daily. In one of his last poems called "The Next War" he concluded presciently that "greater wars" would come where "men believe they war on Death—for Life; not men —for flags." Owen's forecast has been vindicated many times since and, if the sloganeers have their way, could be vindicated again.

Owen's lucid poems about the inherent horrors of war have echoes in the work of other poets both before and since. The astute novelist, essayist and doctor Walker Percy has placed high value on the attitude of poets toward war by stating that "...the poet may admit to being a wounded man, yet point out that a wounded man often has the best view of the battle." Poets in the twentieth century have written of war in the same spirit as Owen, which is a far cry from Tennyson's "Charge of the Light Brigade" where the soldier's duty is but to do or die. Military glory is not celebrated. The focus is on the human cost of war at close quarters—the pain, the futility, the waste.

The chronological leap from World War II to Iraq has not diminished "the pity of war" in terms of losses. One feels the same emptiness and sorrow resurrected in the Iraqi poems of Brian Turner. The theater of war is different, and it's a different decade, but nothing else has changed. Here is Turner's "Ashbah":

> The ghosts of American soldiers
> wander the streets of Balad by night,
> unsure of their way home, exhausted,
> the desert wind blowing trash
> down the narrow alleys, as a voice
> sounds from a minaret, a soulful call
> reminding them how alone they are,
> how lost. And the Iraqi dead,
> they watch in silence from rooftops
> as date palms line the shore in silhouette,
> leaning toward Mecca when the dawn wind blows.

I cite this poem not only for its excellence as a poem, but also because it seems to accept war as a fact of life, unavoidable and recurrent. It was Albert Einstein who said that there would always be war as long as there were men, and Turner seems to reinforce that assumption with specific images. In this sense—and in this sense alone—they are essentially reactions to what war has presented to them—poetic reactions, but reactions nonetheless.

It has been obvious for some time now that a more corrosive evil than war itself is what the *fear* of a possible new war has already done to the American psyche. Some blame politicians for manipulating this fear to their advantage; others blame the defense industries for doing the same for the basest of commercial reasons. Regardless of who is to blame for the exploitation, the damage that is done to the wellbeing of the general population as well as to the nation itself as a constitutional democracy is incalculable. It has made possible the ongoing acceptance of presidentially launched wars with complete disregard for Congress in whom such authority is vested. It has turned a blind eye to government-sanctioned assassinations by drone and otherwise even if the person targeted for assassination is an American. Allied to this is a gradual reduction of civil liberties and the widespread surveillance of the entire population in the name of security. And finally, there is the institution of torture even though information obtained by torture is regarded as highly unreliable and legally inadmissible in court proceedings. Such measures may or may not reduce security threats, but they irrefutably heighten the latent fear they are intended to alleviate in the citizenry.

These Orwellian prerogatives of government are the real threats to our way of life because they undermine the meaning of government in the face of genuine threats. But they themselves are constitutional threats of a much more serious nature. They corrode public trust, and without trust the essence of public life and constitutional behavior corrodes. In her last book, *And Short the Season*, the late Maxine Kumin included poems that defiantly unmasked what these actions were doing to us as Americans. I cite one of four poems dealing with torture, solitary confinement or hooding of prisoners and enforced absence of attorneys for the accused, but the spirit of accusation that underlies the tone of this single poem could easily apply to other abuses, i.e., manipulation of intelligence, assassination prerogatives, domestic spying and the like. What is described in the poem revives the exposed abuses at Abu Ghraib that degraded the United States in the eyes of the world after they were shown to have been ordered by higher authority. The title of Maxine Kumin's poem is "Red Tape and Kangaroo Courts II."

> Soundproof glass between the accused
> and observers on the courtroom
>
> shields what cannot be said

what must be interrupted if the detainees

speak of the dark acts at the dark
heart of what took place during their confinement

for interrogation they held his head in
the toilet and flushed it over and over

for hunger strike they forcefed him until he vomited, then
fed him again until he vomited again

and when he passed out, they doused him awake in a cell
with a steel bunk, no mattress, no blanket.

if we don't talk about the torture
it never happened.

Poems like this reveal what Jane Mayer has perceptively called "the dark side" of America's war on terror. They show that we in fact have assumed the habits that our enemies have ascribed to us. The result is that we have become our own enemy and that the war we fear is not a conflict of arms but a conflict of perceptions already in progress.

Who Quotes Nero?

Poems have birthdays but no funerals. They somehow manage to outlive their creators as well as the times and cultures in which they were written. Why? How?

Numerous answers have been given—some academic, others pedestrian, and still others with silence and a shrug. The common theme that appears in these various answers is that poems or poetic moments in conversation or speeches live on simply because they do. It comes down to memorability. Poetry lives on in those who are affected by it because they cannot forget it even if they try.

Here is a poem that was composed by an Egyptian girl to her beloved in 1500 B.C. Even in translation it has a vibrancy that it must have had more than thirty centuries ago.

> O my beloved
> how sweet it is
> to go down
> and bathe in the pool
> before your eyes
> letting you see how my drenched linen dress

marries the beauty of my body.
Come, look at me.

Some say the poem has endured simply because of its imagery of desire, nothing more. Really? But what of those poems that have nothing to do with love or desire and yet are still with us? Here is a poem from the Greek Anthology translated by Richmond Lattimore. It is one line long and sounds as if it were spoken by a minor military officer who is desperate and surrounded by listless soldiers awaiting orders.

Erxias, where is all this useless army gathering to go?

War has received similar cryptic but equally memorable treatment in our own era in Randall Jarrell's "Death of the Ball Turret Gunner." The ball turret on a B-17 was located on the bottom of the fuselage. It was the first target of enemy fighters attacking the B-17 from below because killing the ball turret gunner would leave the bomber defenseless. It was estimated that the life of a ball turret gunner in battle was approximately eighteen seconds. Here is Jarrell's terse epitaph:

From my mother's sleep I fell into the State,
And hunched in its belly till my wet fur froze.
Six miles from earth, loosed from its dream of life,
I woke to black flak and the nightmare fighters.
When I died they washed me out of the turret with a hose.

I have chosen these three examples at random to demonstrate that memorability does not derive from the subject but by how the subject is poetically seen and presented.

In the saga of Christianity there have been as many derivations of its true meaning as there have been sects and traditions. To some it is a belief in a life to come for the few (the Elect) who have been predestined to be rewarded. To others it is the image of the crucified Christ—an all-too-common prefiguring of the very nature of human life with too little emphasis on grace and redemptive suffering. To Paul of Tarsus it was an invitation to give and accept love every day. He said so in the First Epistle to the Corinthians in words that not only capture but seem to ensue from the very essence of love that most people would affirm. "Yea, though I speak with the tongues of men and of angels and do not have love, I have become like sounding brass or a tinkling cymbal. If I have the gift of prophecy, and know all mysteries and all knowledge; and if I have all faith so as to remove mountains, but do not have love, I am nothing. And if I give all my possessions to feed the poor and surrender my body to be burned, but do not have love, it profits me nothing. Now there abide faith, hope and love, these three, but the greatest of these is love." It is not only the conciseness of the language but the imagery and rhythm of the lines that focus and overwhelm the reader, and it is that art and skill that make Paul's words memorable.

It all comes down to language, the way something is said that is an exact fit for what is meant. It is felt speech. For me one of the best examples of poetic exactness is a short poem by the current poet laureate of Arkansas, Jo McDougall. The title of the poem is "When the Buck or Two Steakhouse Changed Hands." It is a classical example of what happens when a neighborhood lunch room or restaurant is taken over by a national franchise.

> They put plastic over the menus.
> They told the waitresses to wear white shoes.
> They fired Rita.
> They threw out the unclaimed keys
> and the pelican with a toothpick
> that bowed as you left.

I have quoted this poem to friends and strangers on numerous occasions. Every time I finish the third line, I look and see smiles. The smiles tell me that every independent lunch room has its "Rita." She takes the orders, chats familiarly with customers, brings glasses of water without being asked, makes the lunch room feel like home and helps out at the cash register. That reference to Rita and what it implies in a single line create a universal portrait.

These are but a few examples of poems or poetic passages that always create a sense of eternal presence. And those, like me, who often quote them to others perpetuate that presence by doing so.

With literature, as with all the arts, time eventually separates the wheat from the chaff, and what is best endures. The endurance is not commemorative but actual so that the language is as alive as when it was spoken or written. Such language mocks time, which dates every other aspect of life but that. Consider the following three examples. Dead at fifty-two, William Shakespeare lives on in his poetry and the poetic diction of his plays. They have reached millions in multiple countries for over six centuries. Reading a sonnet by Shakespeare or attending one of his plays is not a matter of nostalgia but an experience in the present tense. The words have long outlived the life of their author. The same can be said of the poems of John Keats, who lived only into his twenties. And then there's Robert Frost whose life in decades topped them both and whose poems will certainly exceed his eighty-nine years on this planet. The words of all three of these poets are being quoted into life by someone somewhere even as I write these lines, and that attests to what can only be called their immortality.

The difference between immortality and mere fame or historicity is reflected in the difference between the truly poetic, which is dateless, and that which is confined to dates. If I were to quote Robert Frost's "Two Tramps at Mud Time," the poem by the power of its theme would not end where it stops; the implication of its theme would simply keep widening. Here's how the poem ends.

But yield who will to their separation,
My object in living is to unite
My avocation and my vocation
As my two eyes make one in sight.
Only where love and need are one,
And the work is play for mortal stakes
Is the deed ever really done
For heaven or the future's sakes.

The same guarantee of deathlessness could not be said of others whose names are as well known as Frost's. Who quotes Nero? Who even wants to? Who quotes Genghis Khan, Benito Mussolini, Adolf Hitler or Al Capone with anything approaching what makes them revere and even commit to memory words they want and need to know by heart?

I've noticed the same inclination in the attitude of literate citizens toward politicians they admire. Abraham Lincoln's words at Gettysburg not only defined the very idea of democracy but did it so well that they seem beyond improvement. They are engraved not only at Gettysburg but in the hearts and minds of millions of Americans.

Everyone remembers President Franklin Roosevelt's "We have nothing to fear but fear itself" and his subsequent "Day of Infamy" speech after the attack on Pearl Harbor. Apart from the forensic fact that Roosevelt was a consummate orator, the words in their very brevity captured what a prolonged appeal to hope and solidarity would have blurred. Taken to heart with similar zeal was John F. Kennedy's "Ask not what your country can do for you but what you can do for your country." (At his own inaugural, Richard Nixon eight years later made a self-revealing and predictable change when he altered and debased the line with his own bias to read, "Ask not what your country can do for you, but what you can do for yourselves.") Memorable as Kennedy's original statement was, his speech at the Dáil when he visited Ireland in 1963 was for the Irish unforgettable. Summoning his link with his forebears from

County Wexford, Kennedy at one point recited a verse from a ballad that glorified the resistance of the Irish to British suppression during the "troubles." What made it even more germane was the presence of Eamon de Valera in the audience, the only one of the Irish resistance leaders who was not executed by the British.

> We are the boys from Wexford
> Who fought with heart and hand
> To break in twain the galling chain
> And free our native land.

De Valera and all those around him gave the lines the ultimate applause of reverent, sustained silence.

Language that can actuate the imagination while simultaneously stirring the feelings is language that cannot be ignored. The words are felt, and it is the author's intent and hope that his readers or hearers will feel what he feels. A poet, for example, might caution those addicted to globetrotting by saying as a matter of fact that anywhere they go will become here as soon as they get there. Or the same poet might say to old widowers, who think they will regain their youthful vigor by marrying younger women, that they just might feel even older after they did it. Obviously true, but memorably said...

It has been my experience that it is with children that some of the most memorable words are spoken. Here are a few that I've listed over the years, and I will conclude this brief essay by letting them speak for themselves.

Once my brother-in-law was playfully holding his 6-year-old daughter by the ankles to keep her from moving. Frustrated and knowing that she could not free herself, she said sternly, "Daddy, please let go of my wristlegs." Another totally different but memorable response came to my son, who is a composer and conductor, from a handicapped girl in a high school orchestra when he asked her why she liked music. After a moment, she said, "I like music because I can make it." There was another instance when a young boy and his mother were listening to a weather report on television. It was predicted that there would be a drop in temperature that would be caused by the "wind chill factor." The boy turned to his mother and asked, "Why is it always colder in the windshield factory?" Several decades ago my sister-in-law, who was expecting her third child, was packing a small bag with personal items to take with her to the hospital. Her first son watched and asked her where she was going. "I'm going to the hospital to get your brother." After a brief pause her son asked, "How did he get there?" And finally, there was the time that our dog Oscar died. He was known to and loved by all the children in the neighborhood. Several days after he died one of the neighbor's children approached me on the front porch and asked, "Where's Oscar?" I said that Oscar had died. "When is he coming back?" I explained that Oscar had died and gone to heaven, and that those who have gone to heaven don't come back. The child waited and then asked, "Is Oscar in jail in heaven?"

What Never Could Happen but Did

I was just concluding a four-country lecture tour in the mid-sixties from Lebanon to Jordan to Egypt and Greece sponsored by the State Department. The setting was the American Hellenic Union in Athens where my lecture was scheduled the night after a poetry presentation by the Nobel Awardee George Seferis. When I met Seferis that evening, he asked me where I had appeared previously. After I named the countries, Seferis asked me if I had spoken in English. After I said I had, he added, "You Americans can speak your language anywhere in the world and be understood, but my poems can be understood in my own language only in my own country." I kept thinking of that when I spoke the next night to a much smaller audience than the thousands who had heard Seferis.

After the lecture there was a reception and the usual exchange of compliments and gratitude when a man my age came to my side and said, "Do you want me to save you from this?" He looked like someone who understood how standing in line and responding to compliments could become boring if protracted. He asked again, "Do you want to be saved?" "Yes," I answered, "I think I would."

That said, I watched him pretend to be an official of the Hellenic

Union and lead me out of the auditorium to an adjacent restaurant. He introduced himself as Vassilis Vassilikos and then ordered coffee for the two of us. I recognized the name as that of a short story writer and novelist although I had read none his work since none of it had as yet been translated. The more we talked, the more I realized how conversant he was with contemporary Greek poetry, particularly with that of Seferis and other poets of his generation. Later that evening I asked him if he would be willing to make a brief trip to the United States to present a program of contemporary Greek poetry, and he agreed. (I should add at this point that Seferis himself later came to the International Poetry Forum while he served as Poet-in-Residence at Princeton University).

In retrospect, my meeting with Vassilikos was entirely accidental, but what resulted from it is almost beyond belief.

He and I agreed that a good time for him to come to Pittsburgh would be in late 1966 or 1967. We settled on a date in 1967, and he boarded a plane in Athens to connect in Paris with a transoceanic flight to New York and Pittsburgh.

He never flew farther than Paris.

In April of 1967 a junta of Greek generals replaced the elected government and imposed punishable restrictions on free speech, freedom of assembly, right of dissent and other aspects of a free society. Artists, writers, public figures, intellectuals and all who were considered opponents of the government were arrested, imprisoned, tried or shot.

Had Vassilikos been in Athens at that time, one or the other of these fates would have awaited him. He had just published his novel entitled Z, which was based on the public murder of an outspoken defender of human rights (Dr. Gregoris Lambrakis) and had hardened the hatred of militaristic right-wingers against him. (The murder of Lambrakis had the same kind of effect on the Greek people as the assassination of John Kennedy had on Americans. In Greek the letter Z suggests the verb "he lives.") Though the novel was suppressed in Greece, it was eventually read world-wide and translated into thirty-two languages. (As more time passed, Vassilikos became one of the ten most translated of all Greek authors in history.)

Somehow, he survived in Paris through friends and literary connections during the entire tenure of the dictatorship of the junta and did not return to Greece until 1994. By that time, he was famous throughout the world not only as the author of Z but through the popularity and high quality of a film based on the novel. The distinguished film director Costa-Gavras had read and been deeply impressed by the novel and saw its relevance not only to Greece but to the political turmoil in many countries throughout the world. He cast Yves Montand in the lead role with a supporting cast that included Irene Papas and Jean-Louis Trintignant. He persuaded the widely respected Greek composer Mikis Theodorakis to write the musical score. The film not only received a memorable response internationally but went on to garner the Best Foreign Film honor at that year's Academy Awards ceremony in Los Angeles, the Palme d'Or at the Cannes Film Festival and a Golden Globe. Had foreign films been eligible then for Best Film of the Year, it was widely believed that it would have won.

Because of the reception given his novel and the Costa-Gavras film, Vassilikos was not only internationally famous but self-sufficient economically. For a time, he served as Director of National Television in Athens and later as the Ambassador of Greece to UNESCO. We remained in touch during this entire period, and at one point I asked if he could come to the United States and host a showing of the film Z at the International Poetry Forum where, after the showing, he could respond to questions from the audience. He agreed. He faced a packed house after the showing and answered every question he was asked.

What I finally came to realize (and I'm sure he did as well) was that his original intended flight to Pittsburgh that marooned him in Paris not only saved his life but finally made the film possible. As I've already mentioned, if he had been in Athens when the junta seized power, he would probably never have been heard from again. The only force that can take credit for this would be life itself...the irony and unpredictability of life and its effect on circumstances. In the case of Vassilikos, it would have prevented from happening much of what he today is deservedly known for and by.

He and I stayed less and less in touch as the years and decades passed, but an email from a woman in Athens two years ago changed that. She identified herself as Aspasia Gkioka. She was involved in independent research related to the writings of Vassislikos and came across a poem of mine dedicated to him in a 1968 book of poems entitled *Blood Rights*. This led to my explaining how he and I had met and our linked history since. She then explained that she had two sons enrolled in universities in the United States. She was planning on visiting them and asked if she could visit me also at that time. I told her she would be welcome, and she arrived in due course with both sons. She said that Vassilis was involved with government duties, and that he was seen often in Athens with his wife and daughter. I asked her to remember me to him if she ever saw or met him, and she said she would. In November 2023 I received an email that consisted only of a single line...."Vassilis died yesterday."

From that day until now I have thought of him and of how nothing but coincidence was all we had in common from the time he steered me from a receiving line to a restaurant next to the American Hellenic Union in Athens, of how I invited him to come to Pittsburgh and present a program of contemporary Greek poetry, of how the junta's seizure of the Greek government not only compelled him to cancel the trip but certainly saved him from imprisonment and probable death, of how he became world-famous for a novel and a film based on that novel, of how none of this would have come about if he had remained in Athens and never tried to fly to Pittsburgh. As is often the case with much that occurs by chance for good or ill in life, it was a tale of coincidence, talent, timing and blind luck. What resulted was the birth of a classic novel and film that could just as easily have never happened.

Provence of the Six Winds

To learn to do it. To compact into a prescribed number of words what Smollett, Stendhal, Ford Madox Ford, Henry James, M. F. K. Fisher, Marcel Pagnol, Michael Jacobs, Lawrence Durrell and, most recently and profitably, Peter Mayle needed whole books to do. To re-create the tennis-audience look of sunflowers near Avignon as they follow the daily lob of the sun in uniform obedience. To describe the rinsed and detail-enhancing light that, according to legend, permitted Don Quixote to regain his sanity when he returned to the Spanish equivalent of these latitudes and later attracted Van Gogh, Bonnard, Renoir, Matisse and Picasso. To leave off reading the entablature on the great door of St. Gilles and drive past the grazing fields where the surly black bulls of the Camargue stand and stare like sculpture. To invoke the salad of scents that are yours for the inhaling: jasmine and lavender, croissants at dawn, the seawinds from the Mediterranean, the primal fertility odors in camembert and brie. To pause at St. Laurent du Var and remember as you look seaward that Antoine de St. Exupery vanished without a trace in his Lockheed Lightning south of this coast in 1944. To confront the Pont du Gard for the first time and wonder how few people know the name of M. Visanius Agrippa, the architect who designed the arched two-storied bridge of beige rock. To feel the presence of the past beneath your soles as you negotiate the cobbled, drain-divided streets of Gourdon, Eze, Tourette-sur-Loup, St. Paul de Vence and other *villages perchés*. To be in Uzes on market day and see how the alphabet of colors in bolts of Provençal fabric actually outdoes the natural tints in lemons, eggplants, scallions, tuna, shrimp, corded thighs of lamb and the dull maroon of wet liver. To contrast the latent hedonism you see here with the knowledge that Avignon was the home of seven popes (not all exemplary in a city that shocked Petrarch) and that cloisters, shrines and abbeys are plentiful in a country that has always regarded itself as the oldest daughter of the Roman Catholic Church. To learn that a monastery founded by St. Honoratus on the Iles de Lerins off the coast of Cannes provided Europe with more than 900 bishops and that one of them went to a certain fame in Ireland. To the consternation of all who believe otherwise, a plaque on the wall of the still functioning monastery proclaims that St. Patrick was one of the 900.

All of these descriptive challenges await me as I zoom south from Paris to Avignon on the TGV (*Train à Grand Vitesse* or High Speed Train), foregoing a jet arrival in Nice. After receiving much advice about "how to write about Provence," I have decided that I will proceed like a whale swimming through clouds of plankton, swallowing indiscriminately, digesting selectively. Or I will imitate Diogenes by going wherever curiosity dictates. I will look, listen taste, touch and smell. I will appreciate the contrasts.

Outside the speeding windows of the TGV pass stationary herds of the beef cattle of Burgundy, nuclear power plants, pruned vineyards on terraced hillsides bordering the parallel Rhone (probably a corruption of Rhodes from the time when the first Greeks came to Provence in 600 B.C.), then the soupy warmth of Avignon in July. From the France of Paris to the France of Avignon is an experience in decompression as if the passage is not from one latitude to another but from one culture to another, and, in a sense, it is. In a frequently quoted statement Victor Hugo implied as much when he wrote: "In France, one argues; in Avignon, one kills." It was as if he were speaking of another country.

Ahead of me is a month's tour of Provence, but first I have to deal with Jean-Luc of Avis. I show him my auto rental papers and ask him in French if he speaks English.

"A lee-tle," he answers. This is the French's classic way of avoiding the need to respond to difficult questions by pretending that they know less than they know. Jean-Luc studies the papers and begins "explaining me" that my reservation cannot be for the Saab I have been promised since he has no Saabs. He will find an alternative.

"Is the car air-conditioned? Not ventilated, but air-conditioned?" I ask. I've been to the south of France in July before, and I know what it means to boil behind the wheel.

"But of course," he says as if I've raised a question of honor.

"Are you sure?"

"But of course."

Prior to my dealing with Jean-Luc I listened to a strident conversation between his associate and two Americans arguing in Long Island English about a car that the associate could not produce.

"Here's the paperwork guaranteeing the car," said the first American.

"Guaranteeing," stressed the second American.

"But I do not have the car," said the associate, using the French tactic of becoming icily correct when pressed—not annoyed, just correct. "If monsieurs will be patient, I will make a research."

"We're not leaving here without a car," said the first American.

"If monsieurs will be patient."

While the associate "researched" at his computer, the Americans sulked, huffed and spoke in vicious whispers about Franco-American relations.

"Would monsieurs accept a larger car in the next higher category at the same rate?" asked the associate calmly.

End of controversy. The Americans left happy. Franco-American protocols had been repaired. The associate had done what the French do to perfection—reward after delay. Jean-Luc repeats this procedure with me. I forget my Saab and drive off in a freshly washed Ford Mondeo with only 2,000 kilometers on the odometer.

Looking for the correct entry gate into the walled city of Avignon, I pass directional signs for Arles, Nimes, Aix-en-Provence and Tarascon. The French excel at this kind of road signage, and I feel reassured that I will always be able to find my way to these and other destinations in the weeks ahead. But driving into Avignon was a different story. I had never driven into a walled city before. Inside the walls, I felt that I was behind the dikes that were holding out the soiled seas of this world. I edged forward slowly behind the behinds of pedestrians to whom my car was totally irrelevant. The streets that led to my hotel seemed made for carts rather than cars. At one point I actually brushed the mirror on the passenger side against an open door. I would have similar experiences later in Haut-de-Cagnes and Roussillon where clearances had to be gauged in fractions of inches.

Finally, the Hotel Mirande. It was literally in the very shadow of the Palace of the Popes. On the days that followed I strolled the sloped plaza (the size of a soccer field) that separated the palace from the Institute of Drama opposite where Gérard Philipe served his apprenticeship. Tourists aimed their cameras or video recorders at the austere walls of the palace, at the strategically placed Botero sculptures on the plaza itself, at the organ grinder (a boy of, perhaps, ten) who cranked out Provençal folksongs while his terrier snoozed obliviously on the top of the grinder itself.

But where and what is Provence? Martine Bruel, a graphic artist from Boston but reared in the Var and the Vaucluse where her mother still lives, says, "Provence is a feeling." For her the feeling should include Nimes and Uzes and other places in the Gar and Languedoc. When I demur and point to a map delineating the five departments of Provence as the Bouches du Rhone, Vaucluse, Var, Alpes des Hautes and Alpes Maritimes, she says definitively, "Geographers are not historians." Her view is echoed by James Pope-Hennessy, among others. "The whole area of Provence from the Maritime Alps to the Rhone, from the Dauphine to the sea, is made homogeneous by the universal culture of the olive and the vine, by the language, traditions, ideas and physique of the people who inhabit it.... Though technically in the Languedoc, Nimes and the Pont du Gard belong by cultural tradition to Provence." Such floating definitions are not uncommon. The drawn contours of Provence on the cover of the Michelin Guide, for example, delineate the boundaries to include Nimes in the east, Aix-en-Provence in the west, Lyons in the north and Marseilles in the south.

And what of the Riviera? The cartographers include Nice, but one Frenchmen tells me pejoratively, "Nice is not Provence. Nice was not even a part of France until the last half of the nineteenth century. Nice was Savoy—Italian." The problem is made no simpler by authors. The novels of the great Provençal author Jean Giano suggest that Provence for him was the area around his home village of Manosque. Then there is Ford Madox Ford who loved Provence to the extent that he claimed "if we except Periclean Athens, (Provence) is the only real civilization that the world has yet seen." Nonetheless, he contends that everything west of the Rhone is not Provence, adding that Provence "is not a country nor the home of a race, but a frame of mind." Well, how does one frame a frame of mind? Finally, there are those who say that Provence begins at the Mediterranean and ends at the "olive line"—the line above which olive trees do not grow. Where do these often conflicting definitions leave me? Better to begin with the France of the cartographers but to leave room for poetic license, which permits Provence to be a feeling or an idea without boundaries. If contradicted, I will give a Cartesian shrug and say, "Provence is Provence."

"Provence has been inhabited since the Stone Age," wrote Bergenger-Feraud, the retired naval physician who named the five departments in 1885. Etchings in the Valley of Merveilles alone would seem to substantiate this. But France's significant demographic history begins in the tenth century B.C. with the Ligurians. Four hundred years later the Greeks arrive, colonizing and developing Marseilles (Massalia) as well as Le Ciotat (Kitharista), Hyeres (Albia), Antibes (Antipolis), St. Tropez (Athenopolis), Nice (Nikea) and Monaco (Monoikos). They in turn are followed by the Celts (Arles originates from the Celtic Ar-lath) and the maritime Arabs of the Levant whom the Greeks called Phoenicians. Then came the Romans, whose imprint on Provence (Provincia Romana and Gallia Narbonensis) is the most definitive of all. Intermingle subsequent incursions by Teutons, Vandals, Saracens and Visigoths. Accelerate the centuries of migration, resettlement, invasion and intermarriage, then include 250,000 *pieds noirs* (French colonials) and harkis (pro-French Algerians) as well as Tunisians and Moroccans, and you end with a population mix of blood and cultures that can only be called Mediterranean.

Apart from demographics, what manifests itself constantly in Provence is the imposition of a Christian culture upon a pagan one with the former using the latter for its own enrichment and purposes whenever necessary. I sense this when I visit the deservedly famous Roman theater in Orange—an acoustical marvel backed by the mother of all walls. When I leave, I notice the small chapel of St. Florent in the very shadow of the amphitheater. An accidental or deliberate proximity? If deliberate, why? I will see the same pattern in Arles where the cloisters and chapel of St. Trophime are adjacent to the coliseum-like theater. But nowhere is this more striking than at the Alyscamps in Arles. The paralleling columns of stone sarcophagi lead to the church of St. Cesaire at the end. Was there some need to construct a Christian structure in order to "baptize" the pagan one by having it positioned in the immediate vicinity?

When I mention these proximities of pagan and Christian sites to John Templeton, a retired British admiral who has lived in Provence for more than a quarter of a century, he says, "Why not? Christmas and Easter, after all, are built on pagan feasts. Here the physical evidence of the same tendency is all around us." As he speaks, a Mirage fighter jet, practicing a sub-radar maneuver known as contour-flying, streaks overhead like a burst of summer thunder, reminding everyone that the feast of war changes only in means, not intent. "Actually the people here are more influenced by the weather than by pagan or Christian finalities. Our weather is like that fighter that just passed. It changes sensibilities. When it's marvelous, it's more marvelous than anywhere else, but it's as bad as anywhere when it's bad. Look at what happened in Vaison-la-Romaine. Storms and a flood. The Provençaux are like that. When they're kind, they're kinder than anyone. But there's an underlying violence. Sometimes it just bursts out. Like the mistral. Like the wind."

As I listen, I recall the famous three curses of Provence: taxes, the Durance and the mistral. I cannot help but note how two of the three have to do with nature, which makes me take Templeton's theory seriously.

Later, when I look down from the ash-white peak of Mr. Ventoux or the rust-colored ramparts of Roussillon on what Shakespeare's Burgundy described as "our fertile France," I am overwhelmed by the mix of utility and beauty. The land is plotted for maximum yield. The rock gorges, crevasses, mini-Alps and the impenetrable maquis in the valleys and foothills give way to flawlessly neat farms and vineyards. (What did Petrarch see when he climbed Mt. Ventoux in 1336—the first man to do it?) On the same day I drive to Les Baux. I see the same contrast—the fertility of the flatlands (interrupted by cooperatives where the grape farmers truck their harvests for processing) and the rock ledges and monoliths where Les Baux of the troubadours perches. Fertility and severity. Are these the two poles on which the world of Provence turns?

Somehow the combination of geography, climate, manners, work and temperament have created a seasonal inclination in the Provençaux to celebrate. From Nimes to Menton, from Sisteron to St. Maxime there are festivals, festivals, festivals. There are festivals for mimosa, jasmine, roses, films, jazz, saints, harvests, feast days, celebrities (a Gérard Philipe film festival, for example, in Ramatuelle where Philipe is buried), horses in Sts. Maries de la Mer, pottery, wine poetry (the International Contemporary Poetry Meeting in Tarascon), lemons (the lemons used in the parade floats in Menton are subsequently crushed, boiled into marmalade and bottled for the attendees), accordions, chestnuts, silence (only the French would think of this in the same way as only the French would headline "*Mort d'un Poète*" when Leo Ferme died in the summer of 1993 and relegate the difficulties of the franc to a position of lesser importance on the front page of Nice Matin) and, finally and gloriously, humor (in Aubagne).

Common also in Provence is the interchangeability of fact and legend. Facts often become legends, and legends facts. Whether Mary Magdalene, Mary Salome and the sister of the Virgin Mary ever sailed to the spot so marked at Stes. Maries de la Mer is too immersed in myth to confirm, but the cult of the three Marys exists in the minds of the populations as a historical certainty. Add this to the area's history and sociology, and you have a mixture within a mixture within a mixture. Imagine going to a summer Sunday bullfight in the Roman Coliseum in Nimes where Spanish toreros perform before a population that is defiantly bourgeois, predominantly Protestant and descended from the Huguenots, who successfully resisted the French king in a squabble over the Albigensian heresy. If that's not a potpourri, what is? Compound this by including the recent influx of Algerians, Tunisians, Moroccans and other North Africans who are bringing Islam with them into a country that is nominally Catholic. This has even provoked debate about transforming France's traditional orientation so that it will accommodate two religions. Actually, this is the inevitable fruit of French imperialism in North Africa and elsewhere—a colonialism in reverse. The problem will not go away. What is sown will be reaped even if the sowing and the reaping are the lots of different generations. If this reaches a point in France where Islamic fundamentalism is pitted against French chauvinism, the consequences could be ugly indeed. Chauvinistic or not, the French have no intention of permitting their culture to be adulterated by immigrants who do not integrate. Ironically, however, their latent prejudice against the North Africans does not invite integration as much as it encourages tribalism. What results is suspicion, discord and violence. In parts of Marseilles like Le Cayolle, fights between the police and unemployed North African youths are not uncommon. Such incidents feed the racist appeals of Jean-Marie Le Pen's National Front. It even inspired Valery Giscard d'Estaing, during his presidency, to urge that French citizenship should be determined by French parentage and not merely by proof of birth on French soil—citizenship by womb. This blatantly biological qualification for French citizenship may have been prompted by fear of numbers. Today half of France's 4,000,000 immigrants are North African or from Arab countries. This has prompted the government to attempt to reduce future immigration to zero even though it is openly acknowledged that 100,000 illegal immigrants enter the country annually from North Africa alone. How does one reconcile immigration with national needs, human rights and constitutional principles? This problem will challenge intelligent and cultural leaders for decades to come. In this regard, the responses of Le Pen, who is now a power in Nice as well as Marseilles, and d'Estaing seem reactionary at best.

Putting aside for the moment the problems of immigration and integration, it is hardly surprising that Provence is attractive to outsiders. The geography, the climate, the agriculture and the way of life are inducements in themselves. In addition, the Christianity of the south is less Jansenistic and Cartesian than it is in the north. It is more of the blood, more suited to the senses, more "of this world." For these and other reasons people have come here as invaders, traders, conquerors, visitors, immigrants, transplanted residents or tourists. The list is a long one and includes Celts and Berbers as readily as the floating royalty of Russia, Nijinsky, Gerald and Sara Murphy, Cole Porter, Ernest Hemingway (who expanded a short story called "Mr. and Mrs. Eliot" into a posthumously published novel called The Garden of Eden, centering it in La Napoule), W. Somerset Maugham (who treated Spencer Tracy with hauteur when they were introduced in Cap Ferrat), Van Gogh, Dirk Bogarde for a brief time, Stephen Spender, "Baby Doc" Duvalier (whom I saw lounging languidly with his retinue on the beach in Cannes and lunching on champagne and ice cream), Lebanese who have relocated here since the war, Peter Mayle (whose *A Year in Provence* and *Toujours Provence* are in every bookstore in the area in trade and deluxe editions), Albert Camus, Yves Montand, Jeanne Moreau, Brigitte Bardot, Isadora Duncan (who was strangled on the Boulevard d'Anglais in Nice when her scarf became entangled in the wheel of a sports car in which she was a passenger), Sartre, St. Exupery (who retreated to Le Cagnard in Haut-de-Cagnes for seclusion), Spencer Tracy (who loathed W. Somerset Maugham before and after he met him), a Saudi Arabian prince whose unique car was designed to resemble a camel, assorted English men and women following in the footsteps of Queen Victoria and settling in Cimiez and Grasse. The list is endless.

Regardless of what attracted such a diverse population to Provence, the fact remains that Provence is a part of the world to which people come (however temporarily) rather than from which people go (however temporarily). Ford Madox Ford attributes much of this to spices and the enhancing and seducing effect these have on the cuisine people want to eat here. "Provence is the only country in the world," he writes, "to contain a sufficiency of spices." Provence is a veritable spicery with its native "mint, thyme, tarragon, verjuice, verbena, fennel, lime-flowers, butter-oranges, lemons, absinthe...olives, basil, garlic...pimento...peppers and mustard." Ford then notes that more wars have been fought over spices than over religion but that the Provençaux, though involved in many battles with invaders, "only once in recorded history issued from their borders in an aggressive war." His conclusion is that "Provençal digestions are tranquilized and her populations content to stay at home." In this sense, Provence (contradicting Hemingway's view of Paris) is not "a moveable feast." People must come to Provence to share and experience it. Or to dream of it longingly and praise it in poetry and song. When Keats had intimations of death in England after hearing the song of a nightingale, he longed "for a draught of vintage! that hath been / Cool'd a long age in the deep-delved earth, / Tasting of Flora and the country green, / Dance, and Provençal song, and sunburnt mirth." Peire Vidal, one of Provence's greatest poets, wrote of Provence as one would write of a beloved parent or mentor: "I drink deep into my lungs wind that I know comes from Provence; / From that country everything that comes give me pleasure / And listening to the praises of her I smile. For every word of praise that is said I ask for a hundred / So much I am pleased by the praise of that land. / From the mouth of the Rhone to Valence, between the sea and Durance! / In that noble land did I leave the joy of my heart. / To her I owe the glory that the beauty of the verses and value of my deeds have gained for me, / And as from her I draw talent and wisdom, so it is she that made me a lover and, if I am a poet / To her I owe it."

There are countless other tributes by poets from Fredric Mistral to Yves Bonnefoy. Mistral, who won the Nobel Prize for Literature in 1904, not only praised Provence in his poems but even went so far as to donate all of the Nobel money to perpetuate Provençal letters and culture through the Arlaten Museum in Arles. Bonnefoy, who lived in Provence before accepting a post in Boston, wrote nostalgically about his life there for years afterward. And Rene Char offers this simple, defining tribute in *Leaves of Hypnos:* "This rock-hold of fine people is a citadel of friendship. Everything that blurs lucidity and hampers confidence is banished from this place. We have been wedded once and for all in the presence of the essential."

I discuss this symbiosis of literature and landscape during a meeting with Anne Wade Minkowsky in her re-modeled farmhouse in Les Astiers in the Vaucluse. An Arabist and translator (of the poetry of Adonis, a perennial Nobel candidate), she says, "The influence of the Andalusian Arabs on Provence is considerable. It's quite subtle, however, and it's not frequently acknowledged."

Later I discuss this influence with Ian Meadows, a Scot living in St. Julian de Briola near Carcassonne and an authority on the Arabs in Occitania.

"The origins of the Parsifal legend and that of the Holy Grail come from southern France," Meadows tells me. "Also it's the mother of lyric poetry in the West. It's not only what made Petrarch Petrarch but also what inspired Dante to make Beatrice a symbol for sanctifying grace in The Divine Comedy. Shakespeare's Romeo and Juliet, Donne's love lyrics and even Herrick's poems are in the same tradition. The prototypes of western love originate in Provence as well."

The tradition to which Meadows refers begins with the troubadours, who are the bridge between Andalusian Arab Spain and Provence. The word "troubadour" itself is derived from the Arabic "altarab," which can be roughly translated as a state or mood evoked by beautiful music. The musical poems of the troubadours had as their subject the praise of a beautiful but unattainable woman. This tradition can be traced to Sufism with the woman being addressed as if she were divine, a substitute for God. As man's love for God is unrequiteable in life, so is the lover's love for his beloved.

What the Andalusian Arabs and the troubadours created was a poetry of perpetual desire as opposed to a poetry that stressed gratification. "The longing of the troubadour, always unsatisfied and never exhausted," Giovanna Magi has written, "is the centre (sic) of the whole new conception of poetry and love." In brief, Raimbault d'Orange, Folquet de Marseille, Peire Vidal and other troubadours made poetry and music out of romantic anguish.

When this tradition of the troubadours collided with the poetic tradition of Rome in Provence, which could and did accommodate ribaldry, vulgarity and the copulatory poems of Catullus, the offspring created the schizophrenic basis for courtly love and subsequently for Western love in general. The sung praises of the unattainable and divinized woman—an impossibility in fact—created for a time and possibly for all time the image of a dream-woman. The lover inevitably searched for her in a person other than his wife, she being reserved for bearing and rearing children and house-management—a Catullan hausfrau. Of course, one could never marry the dream-woman under the codes of courtly love since that would make the dram real, and one could not know in advance if the love was transferable. As Denis de Rougemont has written, the result is the ongoing split between passion and conjugal love, between romance and marriage. Observe grand opera or soap operas, and there it is. The element of romance, which is present in all living, is often not integrated or transformed into the dailiness of married life. This compels either mate in a tired or routinized marriage to believe that romance with all its attractiveness, its excitements, its uncertainties and superficial nobility is by definition extramarital. Hence, "affairs," "the other woman," "mistresses," et cetera. The Arabs and troubadours at least had the good sense to believe that romantic love should be unrequited. They knew that reality and satiety were its natural enemies. Better to sing of it than live it.

Ian Meadows documents parallels between the Arab poems of romantic suffering and many of Provençal origin. He notes, for example, that Peire Vidal's search for the wild she-wolf of the Permautier is directly derivative of Ibn Zaldun's for the daughter of the Caliph of Mustakfi in the eleventh century. This in turn is linked to the other Arab legend of the mad lover (Majnun) who searched the desert endlessly for his beloved Leila. It also has affinities with the Celtic persona of Angus. In William Butler Yeats' "Ballad of the Wandering Angus," Angus pursues "a glimmering girl" until he is "old with wandering." Is the connection far-fetched? Not necessarily if you recall that the Celts were long a part of Provence and that Yeats himself, in play and poem, was aware of the Arab influence upon them.

Just as the troubadours transformed the legacy of Arab Andalusía into a language and melody of their own, so did the Provençal weavers invent their own textiles based upon fabrics imported from the Orient. Eventually they created fabrics and patterns that are now identified with Provence and only with Provence. This began when clothes from India were imitated by weavers in Avignon and Tarascon despite a curious papal interdict against the practice. The industry flourished then and flourishes now under the manufacturing labels of Olivades and Soleiado. Stores, boutiques and open markets are stocked with distinctively dyed (one color at a time) and patterned (invariably geometric) bolts that can be transformed into tablecloths, place mats, skirts, blouses, shirts, umbrellas, draperies, cushion and sofa covers, crimped caps on miniature cruets of breakfast jams and jellies, and sock-sized packets that contain herbs of Provence or lavender.

An equally indigenous and related craft that is centered in Cogolin near St. Tropez is the weaving of tapestries, carpets place mats and other domestic textiles. Paul Clavier, the financial director of Tapis de Cogolin, explains during my tour of the factory that his staff of thirty women is in a slack period at the moment, working only four days instead of the usual five. He blames this on the economic climate, not only in France but internationally, but adds that women are paid for five days regardless. Behind him are bins of carded and dyed spools of white, pink, blue, yellow and red wool. All the wool is from France, chemically dyed and then woven by hand in either the old or the modern process. In the old method each woman weaves at a loom, compressing one horizontal thread at a time. In this way she can weave approximately two meters a day of finished fabric (all with geometric and not figurative designs). If she is exceptional, she might even be able to weave three meters. The modern method is to have artists trace a pattern on stretched and mounted backing after which a woman shoots wool threads from a wool-loaded gun into the already sketched patterns. Local artists have been contracted for this purpose, but Clavier possesses additional designs by Leger, Mondrian and other more famous artists. When you thank him for the tour, he tells you that many of his products are distributed in the United States by Brunswick and that some are represented in the "*Maison Blanche.*"

While still in Cogolin, I discover a small factory where smokers' pipes are carved. The owner is Charles Courrieu. Courrieu's son, Thierry, tells me that the Courrieu family has been in the craft and business of handcrafting pipes since 1802. He proudly shows me framed photographs of the "old factory" in the same location taken almost a century ago. Factory is actually a misnomer. Workshops would more accurately describe the two kitchen-sized rooms where the pipes are spun on lathes, bored, balanced, stemmed with ebony or lucite and finally trademarked: "Courrieu Cogolin." All of the briar comes from the root burls of a heather-like bush that grows in the higher altitudes of the Maures so that the raw material is as local as the craftsmen...and one craftswoman. Thierry estimates that his eight employees, the best of whom seems to be the lone woman who bevels and burnishes the pipe bowls and shanks like jewelry on a buffing wheel, turn out 25,000 pipes a year. The prices vary from modest to hundreds of dollars for the artistic, fine-grained models. Thierry adds that there is a large "restoration or reparation" business where broken, impacted or "sick" pipes are set right again. A well-stocked shop adjoins the factory. The whole enterprise shows no signs of depression despite the international movement *contre tabac*. Indeed the pipes of Cogolin are a genuine source of pride for the community as well as for France itself, and the palpable bond between *père et fils* indicates that there will be no petty squabbles at the top.

Another craft identified with Provence is the sculpting of glass, and it is practiced to a masterful perfection by the glassblowers of Biot, which is also famous for being able to harvest more than fifty tons of table grapes per year. From the central workshops of Biot have spun off highly individualized ateliers created by men who learned their crafts as apprentices and then struck out on their own. One of the best of these is Robert Pierini. On a stifling summer afternoon I visit him at his kiln with its adjoining boutique. Pierini is shaping a vase from a head-sized gob of hot glass fixed like a molten Q-tip to the end of a steel pole as long and thick as a broom handle. I watch him turn and tease the vase-to-be out of the gob, firing it again and again in the kiln, cupping it with one hand gloved in asbestos like a lover or sculptor palming a breast, spraying it, scissoring off the excess, beveling and leveling the base, smiling or frowning as the work goes well or stubbornly. He is forty-two, bearded *como un diablo* and built like a soccer goalie. He smiles the inward smile of a man to whom the achievement of perfection is the only human enterprise worthy of man's time and energy. Taking a break from the kiln, he gives you his fax number "in case." The business man in him slowly surfaces but without insistence. He compliments me on my pathetic French as we converse, and I leave feeling as I always feel after I have talked with someone whose work and life are synonymous. I feel that some things are complete in this world.

The abundance of fine craftsmanship in textiles, briar and glass (as well as olive wood) is more than balanced by Provence's wealth in the fine arts. It is not by accident that there are more art museums in Provence than in any comparable area in the entire world. Nor would it be inaccurate to say that many of the greatest artists of this century and before did some of their best work while they lived here. Their legacies have become tangible parts of the areas where they worked. Go to Arles, for example, and the name of Vincent Van Gogh is omnipresent as are reproductions of his paintings on posters, art paper, diaries, appointment calendars and T-shirts. This latter form of exploitation is understandable as avarice's indebtedness to memory, but it is ironic that this Dutchman, who sold but one painting in his short and tragic life, is not represented by a single original painting in Arles or Provence. The irony intensifies when I visit the cloister and clinic of St. Paul in St. Remy just below the stunning Roman ruins at Glanum. It was here that Van Gogh lived and painted after admitting himself for care by the resident doctors. Seeing Van Gogh's room is now forbidden. Even the bronze bust of Van Gogh by Zadkini was stolen by vandals in 1989. The pedestal that displayed the bust near the aisled entrance to the cloister remains. Beside it is a photograph of the bust together with a note in explicit French excoriating the thieves who stole it. It is as if Van Gogh's spirit is present only by hearsay.

What Van Gogh meant and means to Arles and St. Remy is replicated in the link between Paul Signac and St. Tropez, Henri Bonnard and Le Cannet, Pierre-August Renoir and Cagne-sur-Mer where he painted to the end with paintbrushes taped to fingers stiffened like sticks by advanced arthritis, Paul Cezanne and Aix-en-Provence, Jean Cocteau and Menton, Henri Matisse and Nice as well as Vence, Marc Chagall and St. Paul de Vence, and Pablo Picasso and Vallauris, Antibes, Cannes and Mougins. These names are not merely a litany of the greatest artists of our time. These are the authors of paintings that unveiled Provence internationally to all those who learned of it first through their art. This proves again that most people do not truly see what they're seeing until it is seen for them in prospect or retrospect by the artist-seer. You cannot peruse the countryside around Aix-en-Provence or the whale-head contour of Mt. Victoire without seeing them as Cezanne saw them. The same holds true of Chagall and St. Paul de Vence. Look down from any window on the little cemetery at its base, where Chagall is appropriately buried, and you find yourself looking with Chagall's eyes at the aboveground stone gravemarkers festooned with ribboned bouquets, vased lilacs or neatly cellophaned roses, jonquils or carnations.

Not far from where D. H. Lawrence died in Vence, I visit the Blue Chapel of the Rosary that Matisse created to thank the Dominican nuns who cared for him in their infirmary there. Standing before the raised, angled altar, I understand how spirituality can infuse art. It's in the simplicity of lines on the walls and a corresponding simplicity in the recently exhibited vestments which Matisse created for celebrants to don there. I see in these the same sure hand that created the "Nude with Orange" in the Pompidou in Paris; the subject changed but not the talent. The final tribute I feel obliged to pay after visiting the chapel is that Matisse, a non-believer who was at home with hippy odalisques in wanton sprawls, could and did create a space that actually induces prayer.

And then there is the Provence of Picasso—a Provence Mediterraneanized by this Catalan genius to whom France was an adopted country. But what Provence gave to Picasso, it received in return a hundredfold, not only in the work he bequeathed to it but in what his art and generosity did for it. Like Mistral before him, Picasso contributed some of his largesse to support the Reattu Museum in Arles. And there was the way he reciprocated the kindness of the director of the Chateau Grimaldi who let him use the chateau for half a year in 1945. In appreciation Picasso bequeathed most of the work he did there to create what is now the Picasso Museum.

Picasso's flamboyance engendered numerous legendary stories, some apocryphal, some not. Rumor has it, for instance, that Picasso moved out of his home in Cannes because a new apartment complex blocked his view of the sea. The daughter of his son Pablo now lives in it. Another anecdote is that Picasso and Françoise Gilot, his companion at the time and later the wife of Dr. Jonas Salk, had rented a villa for the summer from a French general. When the general returned, he found the walls splashed with paint. Picasso apologized, explaining that he and Françoise Gilot were "sloppy painters." To compensate, Picasso offered the general any painting of his choice free of charge. Despite the fact that Picasso's paintings at the time were selling for hundreds of thousands of dollars, the general is reported to have said, "No, thank you. I don't like your work."

The most serendipitous marriage between Picasso and Provence occurred when the ceramists Georges and Suzanne Ramie of the Madoura factory in Vallauris invited Picasso to consider clay as an artistic medium. Picasso worked at the factory for one day (July 1, 1946), then returned one year later to the day to forge an alliance with the Ramies that extended for twenty-five years in all. Some of Picasso's work in ceramics is on daily display in the Madoura factory and boutique. A complete historical catalogue of his total creation shows you dishes with human faces, platters on which toreros dare ceramic bulls, water pitchers whose handles are the ears of faces on the sides. The catalogue is the work of Alan Ramie, the son of Georges and Suzanne Ramie. Not a ceramist himself, Alan Ramie manages the various Madoura enterprises and is aware that he is involved not merely with a business legacy but "with history itself." He explains that Picasso himself prescribed the numbers for the limited editions he created in collaboration with Suzanne Ramie. Many are no longer available for sale. Those still for purchase have prices ranging from $500 to the astronomical. Asked if I might see the master ceramists at work (there are only three), Alan Ramie smiles and shakes his head no. No observers are permitted—"*jamais*."

When I leave the Madoura factory and walk down Avenue Georges Clemenceau where the numerous pottery shops show no signs of depression, I pass the Avenue Pablo Picasso. Is this Vallauris' perfect tribute to a man who redeemed its major craft from gradual decline and did more for Vallauris than Georges Clemenceau ever dreamed of doing? Of course, I cannot forget that Picasso painted the Chapel of Peace here in 1970 after numerous exhortations. The war panels of the painting seem repugnant to me, but why should I have assumed that war should generate beauty? And he also donated a sculpture called "Man with Goat" after it was inexplicably and stupidly rejected by the city officials of Antibes. Picasso insisted that the statue be situated in the midst of life. And it is. Visit the open market in Vallauris, and there it stands amid radishes, eggplants, cucumbers, tomatoes, cantaloupes, hucksters and housewives. I assume that dogs can urinate on its base at night, exactly as Picasso said he wanted dogs to do.

But Picasso's most memorable contribution to Provence was to use a medium dug from the earth of Provence itself and transform it into objects where beauty and utility are one. You might even say that he perpetuated a craft that evokes the divine if one is willing to identify God as the original clay sculptor. In this spirit Georges Ramie's tribute to Picasso, with all its baroque elegance, seems the most fitting not merely because it is personal but because it is timeless: "With fitting reverence he approached this magical material, so sensitive to the mere stroke of the thumb yet so implacable in its reactions to the least variations of humidity, so stubborn in the hands of the uncomprehending, yet so docile when treated with respect, a material so fragile while it is still in the shaping, totally dazzled from its recent metamorphosis to become from then on incombustible and imperishable, still to be purified by the terrible ordeal of fire. For here, indeed, this substance of so precious a humility becomes, by its permanence, the truest bearer of the message of mankind; however far back in time one goes, the evidence of humanity from the earliest epochs reaches us, not engraved in stone which crumbles to dust and erodes, not cast in metal which rusts and powders, but on little tablets of clay, with graphic signs as expressive today as when beneath the stylus of the scribe who traced them."

In due course, art museums followed the artists into Provence, and today they constitute a feast of feasts for amateur and professional alike: the Leger in Biot, the Fragonard in Grasse, the Chagall, the Dufy, and the recently refurbished Matisse in Nice, the already mentioned Picasso Museum in Antibes, the Renoir in Cagne-sur-Mer, the atelier of Cezanne in Aix-en-Provence, to name only the most prominent among multiples of other less individualized collections.

The two museums that intrigue me most are the Fondation Maeght in St. Paul de Vence and the Museum of the Annonciade in St. Tropez. The Fondation Maeght is really a stroll in the open air in the company of work by Pol Bury (a fountain of shifting silver tubes that tip and empty endlessly as a continual flow of water dictates), Calder, Chagall, Miro, Arp and Giacometti, whose gaunt striders resemble naked penitents marching eternally toward God. All of these co-populate a park of trees, lawns and incomparable cool shade. The entire space was designed by the Catalan architect Jose Luis Sert, but the real instigator was Andre Malraux, who persuaded Aimé Maeght to create and subsidize it. There is a rock-walled building complete with topping domes that houses the paintings, including a huge, dancing canvas by Chagall, a boutique and a theater. But the unique beauty of the place is its leaf-canopied openness where one can amble or pause beneath umbrellas of pine and murmur an inward hello to sculptures and carvings that suddenly seem like one's closest friends.

The Museum of the Annociade in St. Tropez exists in the very midst of bustle—a shrine of classical elegance beside the docked and softly bobbing yachts on one side and the brasseries, hair salons, card shops, pharmacies and the tourist-jammed streets on the other. The present curator is Jean-Paul Monery, who did graduate work in Chicago on minimalist art and was a curator in Grenoble before coming to St. Tropez. Dissatisfied with St. Tropez itself, he has nonetheless written an opulent catalogue of the museum, which has a lot to be opulent about, plus a Gallimard guidebook for the entire area. Two names dominate his monologue as he describes the museum and its holdings—Georges Grammont, an industrialist and philanthropist who assumed the responsibility and expense of remodeling the chapel (originally La Chapelle de Notre Dame de l'Annociade, built in 1510) into a museum in 1936, and Paul Signac, who came to St. Tropez by yacht in 1892, settled there for twenty years and invited many of his fellow artists to work there for varying periods. Signac's talent and influence plus Grammont's philanthropy almost fifty years later have given the world one of the finest collections of Fauvist and other avant-garde paintings in one of the most tastefully restored spaces in France.

Monery explains certain voids in the collection: "Only half the collection is in the museum at one time. The absent half is on loan or tour." I pass two life-sized bronze female nudes by Aristide Maillol, and I observe how Maillol's nudes are invariably without shame, exaggeration or vanity. Monery pauses before Pierre Bonnard's "Nude in Front of a Fireplace," one of the many paintings in which Bonnard's wife served as his model. I ask Monery to explain as an art historian why Madame Bonnard, on the evidence of the paintings alone, seemed to enjoy the condition of total nudity at home. Monery looks surprised. "But don't you know she had a condition..." He rubs the back of his hand. "How do you say in English? Dermatological? She had a skin condition. She could not tolerate even a tissue on her skin. So she preferred to be naked in her own house." The result is that Bonnard simply painted her as he saw her.

Of course, there are smaller museums and ateliers all over Provence. One that deserves special mention is in Vence—the VAAS gallery and workshop in the restored art studio of Jean Debuffet adjacent to what used to be his home. This is the fulfillment of a dream of Marion Duteurtre, who sold her gallery in Milan to create this space for the exhibition of new art, including the dramatic sculptures of Max Squillace and other Italian and French artists.

But the creation of beauty is not only the prerogative of artisans, writer and artists in Provence. There are also the chefs. And the perfumers.

The cuisine of Provence, differentiated early on from other French cuisine by the Provençal option of using olive oil and garlic, is derived from a bountiful agriculture and *fruits de mer*. Walk through any of the open markets, and you pass a cornucopia of all raw materials that make good chefs salivate when they personally choose the day's foodstuffs: sagittal slices of dourade, pop-eyed loup beside flat-eyed sole, cheese by the loaf or wheel or wedge, barrels of mussels, overflowing bins of fresh green peppers, bunched parsley, potatoes in mesh sacks, cherries and table grapes asprawl, pyramids of the three P's of Provence (*pommes, pêches, poires*—apples, peaches, pears), baguettes, croissants, corked glass quarts and gallons of pellucid olive oils with a sprig of herb immersed in each bottle, bushels of light green melons that have the taste of cantaloupe raised to the umpteenth power. Such open markets abound in every village, town and city. In the hands of chefs like Jacques Chibois of the Gray d'Albion in Cannes, Jean Andre Charial of the Beaumaniere in

Les Baux, Dominique Ferriere of the Chateau St. Martin above Vence, Jean-Ives Johany of Le Cagnard in Haut de Cagnes, Jacques Manimin of the Hotel Negresco in Nice, Alain Ducasse of the Hotel de Paris in Monaco and the deservedly famous and widely revered Roger Vergé of Le Moulin de Mougins in Mougins, the fruits, vegetables, fish and meats of Provence are capable of being transformed into masterpieces for the eye as well as the palate.

French chefs are not only kings in their kitchens. They have the standing of culinary artists in a country where gastronomy is taken seriously. Jacques Maximin, for example, received one of the highest awards the national government can bestow, and the rarely given three-star Michelin rating is worn like a badge of honor by Michoo and Lulu Barel at Le Cagnard in Haut-de-Cagnes as well as by Alain Ducasse and Roger Vergé. In France such citations are roughly equivalent to secular canonizations. Perhaps it derives from the Gallic belief that dining is the only human activity that activates all of the five senses simultaneously. Diners see the food, smell it, taste it, touch it and enjoy the conversation of their fellow diners—all at the same time. Therefore, the great French chefs do not believe that dining should be taken lightly, despite the intrusions of McDonald's and Quik's into civic life. Beside the name of Escoffier, the master French chef from Provence whose name on sauces and cookbooks is known throughout the world and who has a museum commemorating his career in his birth place at Villenuve-Loubet, the fast fooders seem temporary. To the French and the gourmet-cognoscenti everywhere the names of Escoffier and his successors are as well known as Nostradamus, Emile Zola, Alphonse Daudet, the Marquis de Sade, Garibaldi, all of them fellow Provençaux.

One afternoon I discuss restauranteurism at Les Muscadins in Mougins with Edward Bianchini, the Philadelphia-born director and manager of the hotel and restaurant. I begin by telling him that I noticed the restaurant was filled to capacity on the previous night when I ate there.

"That took four years to develop," he says. He speaks slowly, as if reliving each of the four years. "Originally we opted for highly priced dinners, but I fought for reasonably priced complete meals, well presented and well served. For me this is the key to restaurant dining in Provence in the future. And, of course, it is essential to have a good chef."

Later I meet the chef, Noel Mantel. He has just prepared a special lunch of risotto with truffles, filets of mullet sprinkled with crushed olives on a bed of franc-thick zucchini slices and a saddle of lamb ebbed with beans, onions and shallots. He tells me that he has studied cooking from the age of fourteen and that he served his apprenticeship in the best hotels in Nice and St. Tropez. Every day he buys all the vegetables, fruits, fish and meat for Les Muscadins and prepares the menus. He likes working in a small hotel where his authority and responsibilities are not restricted except by the discipline of the work itself. I remember how Bianchini stressed the crucial importance of a good chef to restauranteurism. The shy, quiet-spoken and precise young man opposite me looks vocationally at peace. And confident. And competent. He is twenty-four years old.

Among the numerous outstanding chefs in the south of France there is general agreement that the master chef is Roger Vergé. Together with Paul Bocuse in Lyons, Vergé has given French cooking an international stature that has enhanced tourism in the area. Many restauranteurs credit Vergé with focusing attention on Provence as a center for good food, and many of the leading chefs apprenticed with him early in their careers.

Preparing to meet Roger Vergé in Le Moulin de Mougins, I wish my knowledge of his books was more extensive. I know that his *Cuisine of the Sun* sold more than 100,000 copies in its English edition alone. I know that Vergé has subsidiaries in Disney World's Epcot and in Japan. I will learn that he has an ongoing cooking school in Mougins as well as a second restaurant—L'Amondier, a boutique for his oils and other condiments and a special outlet for his trademarked wines.

In person Roger Vergé impresses me as a man who wears his honors lightly. With his white hair and white mustache, he could pass as someone's French uncle from the interior. But he converses with the ease of a man accustomed to interviews and not in the least hesitant to share what he knows. Because of numerous trips to the United States, his attractively accented English is idiomatic.

"To remain fresh we change our menu five times a year. For the business men's luncheon we change every week. Right now the economy is not as good as before. The *monnaie* is still there, but the people do not spend as much. This is why I have a less expensive menu at L'Amondier." He pauses to take a telephone call, which he handles with the ease and confidence of a man who makes pivotal decisions in his business habitually. "Today too many people ask the children not to be in the kitchen Why? I think children should be in the kitchen if they prefer. I am a chef today because my Aunt Célestine gave me a stool to stand on so I could watch her and help her in the kitchen." Another telephone call, which he terminates with polite dispatch. "For me cooking is like the lines of a drawing. But the sauce is the color. You divide good chefs from ordinary chefs by the sauce. A good chef must be a good saucier."

Later he leads me on a brief tour of the reconstructed mill known as Le Moulin de Mougins. "It has taken me twenty-five years to make what you see." There are original paintings and sculptures (one a compressed cube of old copper cooking pots) by Miro and Caesar. There is a photograph of Salvador Dali. There, one of Picasso. "Picasso rarely came, but I let him park his car in the lot." On the glass walls of an aperitif room are signatures of celebrities of note: Yves Montand, James Coburn, Anthony Quinn, Audrey Hepburn, and Elizabeth Taylor, to name a few. During the Cannes film festival in 1993 Elizabeth Taylor hosted an AIDS benefit dinner at Le Moulin for four hundred guests (including Michael Douglas, Sylvester Stallone, Jack Lang, Louis Malle, Kenneth Branagh and an unbraceleted Adnan Kashoggi) in cooperation with Vergé. "Of all these actors and famous people, my favorite was Danny Kaye. He always came right into the kitchen. In the last of his life he gave everything to UNICEF. He was very generous. He always wanted to share. And I believe like him. Why are we here except we share?"

He talks briefly about a Peruvian girl he has adopted, about his recent friendship with Sharon Stone ("a good actress, but sometimes she has bad parts"), about the need for the constant diversification of menus. When I leave, he invites me to return for a meal as his guest. I tell him I'll take a rain check. He frowns. The term is new to him. After I clarify the meaning, he smiles, shakes my hand and says, "If we have rain or if we have no rain, come back. I will remember you."

I am surprised to learn, after many inquiries and investigations, that France's leading and most profitable export is perfume. Flowers are next, with high tech, textiles and automobiles lower on the list.

The perfume industry actually owes its existence to a woman. To be more specific it owes its existence (as well as its continued existence) to the human nose. The original nose belonged to Catherine de Medici. After a visit to the area around Grasse, she suggested to the glovemakers there that the glove leather should be perfumed to counter its rank smell. They obliged. Instead of remaining glovemakers, they came to identify themselves as glovemaker-perfumers, then perfumer-glovemakers and finally just perfumers. The face of Helen of Troy may have "launched a thousand ships," but in this case a woman's nose, albeit the nose of the destined wife of the king of France, launched an industry.

Centered in Grasse, which is the world capital of perfume, the perfumeries of Fragonard, Gallimard, Molinard and others have made French perfumes synonymous with chic throughout the world. Perfumes have been created in other cultures, i.e., the Egyptian, Greek, Roman and Levantine, but Grasse established its pre-eminence by mixing alcohol with the basic oils and floral essences to give the scents greater stability and longevity. Recently some chemicals have supplemented a few of the organic ingredients (Java patchouli oil, Indian ginger, vanilla, aniseed, ambergris, deer musk, civet from Ethiopian cats and sandalwood, to list the most prominent). To make perfumes of the highest quality from this alphabet of ingredients is not a matter of potluck. It is a genuine science as well as a multi-million-dollar-a-year business.

It all begins with a "nose," the name used in the trade to identify someone whose sense of smell is acute and who has the talent to create new scents by intermarrying existing ones in different combinations. Of approximately three hundred "noses" throughout the world, fifty are in Grasse. To become an official "nose" one must attend a school for "noses" in Versailles. Two years of chemistry are required for graduation, further stressing the scientific core of the profession.

The president and director general of the Fragonard perfumery is Dr. Patrick Fuchs. Although he inherited the factory from his father, he has the requisite credentials for his position. He studied with Nobel Awardee Dr. Robert Burns Woodward at Harvard and has a doctorate in chemistry. He tells me in his air-conditioned office, while hundreds of tourists and schoolchildren are touring the factory just beyond his office door, that his father insisted on his attending Harvard so that Fragonard could be kept abreast of all scientific developments related to the making of perfume. His father spoke from experience, having created a best-selling perfume for Elizabeth Arden called "Blue Grass."

"My brother Gilles did not want to be a perfumer," says Dr. Fuchs. "He has a doctorate in law from Oxford. But then he married the granddaughter of Nina Ricci. So now he is the president of Nina Ricci. One of life's ironies."

I learn from Dr. Fuchs and his staff that the making of perfume in many ways parallels the making of wine. Wine, by the way, is also an industrial staple in Provence with individual wines being identified with individual towns or regions. Provençal wines, even in the Var, are not in the class of the wines of Burgundy and Bordeaux, but they are not dismissable—the rosé of Tavel, for example. As tons of grapes are needed to create good wines, so are abundances of flowers required to create the essences from which perfumes are made. Archibald Lyall calculates that the "coast produces some twenty thousand tons of mimosa, carnations, roses, jasmine, mignonette, narcissi, jonquils, tuberoses, and violets a year." In Antibes alone more than 9,000,000 square feet are devoted to the growing of flowers. This is roughly the equivalent of one hundred city blocks.

Distillation soon makes short work of all this tonnage. Over two thousand pounds of jasmine, for example, are required to create thirty-four ounces of the neroli or essence of jasmine. Similarly, the required number of roses needed to make two and one quarter pounds of rose essence is 10,000,000 roses, approximately one ton. Two thousand pounds of jasmine! Ten million roses! I try imagining such quantities in terms of feathers or ping-pong balls and then give up. And it all boils down to two pounds of essence. Moreover the jasmine and roses must be picked between 4:00 a.m. and 11:00 a.m. so that the fragrance will not be lost to the sun at its meridian and thereafter. A similar care is required in the watering of the plants prior to picking. The watering must be done at night by men in masks who cannot have eaten garlic or onion previously for fear that the scent will be inhaled by the flowers. No wonder that a pound of essence has a price roughly equivalent to its corresponding weight in gold. What an industry hath Catherine de Medici wrought! Beautiful and sweet-smelling in the blooming, providing employment in the harvesting and processing, and garnering profits in the marketing! The entire cycle strikes me as self-sustaining, self-perpetuating and derived from the environment itself. And all for the benefit of Grasse, Provence and France.

I am standing on one of the parapets of Èze, a perched village that gives you a view of the eastern reaches of Provence as far as Menton in one direction and Antibes in the other. I wonder what it is about this part of the world that has drawn people to want to paganize themselves here. Is it because, as I've already noted, Christianity here is less Pauline so that it permits an easier commerce between the flesh and the spirit, a more sensuous and even more sacramental view of life and an acceptance of it on those terms—unsublimated and welcomed? Is it because the

French insistence upon individual taste as the bedrock of social life has its ultimate flowering here? Or is it simply because this is a culture without a false bottom, physically speaking? For those who believe that a man is just a mind, life starts from the top of the head and ends with the chin. For Puritans, life ends at the waist. In Provence it includes everything from the top of the head to the soles of the feet—a total view that has created a way of life that it reflects honestly.

This is not to romanticize the place. All anyone has to do is read Marcel Pagnol's *Jean de Florette* and *Manon of the Springs* or have seen the excellent films that were based on them to get a hint of the mendacity and avarice and venery that lie just below the surface. But such negatives exist wherever man exists. Told by many to be watchful of my valuables during my stay in Provence, I once hurried back to my car where I had parked it fully loaded after having left the key in the car door. Approaching the car and expecting the worst, I saw a young man approaching me with the key in his hand. "Monsieur," he asked, "are you searching your key?" He handed it to me unquestioningly, smiled modestly when I thanked him, shrugged off an offer of lunch as a small reward and left. Nothing in the car had been disturbed.

Still I can't overlook the disagreeable: the glitz of the Noga Hilton in Cannes, the acknowledged networking of the French Mafia from Marseilles into the interior, the seediness of the politics of Nice that Graham Greene publicly exposed and excoriated in *J'Accuse* in 1982 shortly before he died in Antibes, the pollution of the Mediterranean which a consortium (France, Italy, and Monaco) is desperately trying to reverse, the undisguised up-pricing in season of everything from sun-block nipple cream to a dish of strawberries.

But the real Provence is for those who trust in and hunger for the truths of the body and who discover these truths by surrendering to them. Provence does not reveal itself to the disembodied mind. It responds to those who see the world through the senses. It's what one feels when one views the Gorge of Verdon, France's Grand Canyon without the vastness. It's one's response to the long trek to Rocquebrune where Winston Churchill vacationed and William Butler Yeats died. I search Rocquebrune's hilltop cemetery until I find amid the baroque and bourgeois graves the blue, flat natural-stone marker on which is scratched in French: "Here lies Eduard Jenneret, known to the world as Le Corbusier." It's what is able to accommodate John Wayne's former villa in Antibes with its cowboy-hat roof and the restored Chateau St. Martin with its precise and priceless elegance. It's standing before the grave of Albert Camus in Lourmarin with its blackened stone marker on which his name is centered in capital letters along with the dates of his stay on this earth: 1914-1960. Other visitors follow me there as I am following those who preceded me. I think of thirty-three years of visitors—the living's ultimate tribute to greatness. It's sitting at a sidewalk table on the Cours Mirabeau in Aix-en-Provence. I am eating melon and sipping café au lait and appreciating the legacy of Good King René who planted the seeds for this university city in the fifteenth century. It is passing a small alley in Golfe Juan that is marked inconspicuously as the beginning of the Route Napoleon. It is visiting the Castle de Saint-Privat at the Pont du Gard where Richelieu stayed for a week to make allies of the owners his kind could not defeat. The current owner, Mrs. Jean-René Fenwick, is presently engaged in a legal skirmish with the government to keep its encroachments at bay. No counterpart of Richelieu has thus far been dispatched to pacify Mrs. Fenwick. The castle has a flavor of resisted decay while its gardens resemble the set of an Antonioni film. Still it is more authentic than the castle at Ansouis where mounted military portraits, swords and general overdoneness makes you wish for a new Rousseau to turn such puffery upside down. As I am leaving the estate, I notice a number of bathers who are swimming down river from the Pont du Gard or lounging on the irregular shores. In one secluded section a man and a woman, totally naked, are caressing, writhing and kissing one another in complete indifference to the world at large. I wonder how long Mrs. Fenwick can defend herself and her estate against these more proximate encroachments. Or even if it matters. It's standing in the beige-rock chapel of the Abbey at Thoronet and letting the clash of silence and sunlight give you a different sense of your very self—a more resonant one as if you've suddenly been underlined for emphasis. It's walking the interminable beaches of Ramatuelle and Pampalone where nakedness and near nakedness evoke nothing but indifference. Bathers do not seem mistakenly unclothed but simply and frankly nude. It's walking in Èze. The village cats are sunning themselves on warm rocks. You pass two plaques in the cemetery with French male names on them. Under each is the succinct phrase: "Victime de Nazis." In other places in Provence you will see a street named after someone whose name means nothing to you. The name is followed by the word: "Resistant." This is the modest French way of memorializing the Resistance. A small detail, but significant. It's passing St. Raphael and realizing that the invasion of the Riviera happened in this very vicinity in 1944 and not at Nice where the Nazis were expecting it. It's coming to understand that Provence is indeed a "feeling" as much as it is a place that invites and rewards re-visiting. "I could never let a year go by without traveling there for a few weeks at least. Provence is a taste or more correctly a passion which once contracted cannot be cured," wrote James Pope-Hennessy, one of Provence's best biographers. And Bo Niles, the author of *A Window on Provence*, responded in a similar spirit when she wrote about her stay there near Menerbes: "I love the fragrances: lavender, of course, and rosemary. The colors—even if they are bleached by noon; at sunrise and sunset they are exquisite and intense. I love the trees: olive, cypress, plane trees, cherry, and the vegetables, abundant in the markets and garden. The sound of cicadas. The long days."

Mysteries always elude definition in the same way that great paintings seem unframeable even when they are framed. Such is Provence, elusive but true and real as the wind. Or rather the six winds: the *levante* from the east, the *gregaou* with its hail, the northerly *tramontana*, the two sisters from the south, the *sirocco* and the *libeccio*, and, finally, the *mistral*, which originates in the Alps and rushes down the Rhone Valley like an invisible avalanche.

The first time I encountered a mistral was when I was in Avignon. My wife and I were strolling toward our hotel when the evening breeze suddenly seemed to stiffen and then change key, as if in response to a direct order. Within minutes we had to lean our bodies forward just to keep our balance. The knifing, slashing gusts careened though the labyrinthine streets of that walled city as if the very air were in flood. Blown-down leaves swirled against store windows and into gutters, where they huddled like terrified sparrows. Then the mistral climaxed, axing down branches and cartwheeling signs though the deserted square. Those signs that the mistral could not unhinge slammed against their mounts again and again, like sailcloth snapping and shredding in a hurricane. The wind settled—a threatening calm—and then charged back as an enraged bull might charge after a respite. And all the while, the mistral whined and whistled like a chorus of flutes played by the insane.

The mistral, whose name comes from *magister*, the Latin word for master, is a distinctive part of Provençal life, punctuating the region's otherwise congenial climate. It appears throughout the year, unpredictably and without warning.

The force of the mistral is generated when the dry, cold Alpine winds above the northern Rhone valley clash with the warm winds on the Alps' southern side. If there is a drop in barometric pressure, the warm winds yield, and the chilly gusts come barreling down the length of the Rhone valley, not stopping until they reach the African continent.

Short of being caught in one, the most immediate way to learn about the mistral is to talk with residents—permanent ones if possible, seasonal if not. The permanent residents invariably begin with the conventional wisdom. They say that it is a "mud eater" whose arid currents suck up puddles from fields and dirt roads. And they claim that it blows itself out in multiples of three if it begins during the day (three days, six days, and so on) but lasts only long enough to be an annoyance if it rises by night.

What the mistral is most noted for is its ability to put people on edge. It makes people nervous. It causes the eyes to smart and tear. Stendhal called it the "greatest drawback" to a stay in the south of France. And it's bloody loud. This probably explains why the shutters on Provençal windows seem thicker than shutters elsewhere. Nothing decorative here. However hospitable the appearance of unshuttered windows may be to the outside world, the shutters can close up a house like a box when the mistral passes through, sealing out both sight and, one hopes, sound.

There is an island in the Mediterranean (possibly Sardinia) where the inhabitants refer to their version of the mistral as "the whip." The figure is apt, since a genuinely strong wind lashes nature—man included—into submission. Since no one likes to be enslaved, a wind can make rebels out of those it subdues. It is resented. It creates defenses and accommodations. There are, for example, almost no stone belfries in the south of France, the theory being that the mistral will eventually dislodge the stones. The Provençal alternative is the bell cage, in which the bell is hung and swung and rung. The iron bars of the cage permit the wind to blow through and dislodge nothing at all.

The personal counterpart of such accommodation is resignation. One hotel proprietress near Vence looked puzzled when I asked her for her most vivid memory of a mistral—any mistral. "There was a tree that was blown down last year, and I think we lost a few shingles." She gave a French shrug—the kind that suggested how minor a place the mistral had in her scheme of things.

After the mistral has had its three-day, six-day, or nine-day fling, it leaves everything with a rinsed look. I noticed this the day after I experienced my Avignon mistral. While I was driving toward Uzes, I saw that the sky seemed to have been washed as clean as a windshield. The streets and roads shone. The formerly passive facades of buildings and houses actually seemed to be asserting themselves. The grass was definitely greener, but many trees along the road were permanently bent toward the south after decades of being pummeled by repeated mistrals.

To speak finally of the mistral is to borrow the spirit conveyed by the aforementioned French shrug. After all, Provence is a part of the world that is blessed with fertility, a predominantly temperate climate and a special Mediterranean light. Its beauty, excellent cuisine and civilized pace attract visitors from everywhere and keep faithful residents from leaving. Perhaps the mistral is the counterbalance. Its annoyances only intensify our immense appreciation of Provence's many natural gifts by reminding us that nature can intervene at times and places of its own choosing, even in gardens reminiscent of Eden. And when it does, we become like the classical Romans, who believed in the virtue of patience and perseverance in the face of what one cannot control. We accommodate. We shrug. We go on living.

The mistral and its five fellow winds seem to be symbolic of Provence. They blow where and when they will. Shaping and forging a people as well as a climate and a geography. If they cannot be confined by lines on a map, it is because they are as elusive as mysteries. Mysteries can never be imprisoned within a definition. They are knowable only when they are acknowledged and appreciated and loved. That is how it is with Provence. And that is how it should be.

Is Life Ahead or Within?

After meeting his doctor for his annual checkup, a 70-year-old patient told the doctor, "Checkups or no checkups, we all have to die one day. It's just a question of when." The doctor shook his patient's hand and said, "Not when, but how."

That brief exchange reveals not only two different attitudes toward life but two different views of death as well. On the one hand there is the patient's view of life as a time with a statute of limitations. His concern is with longevity. He concedes that death is in everyone's future, but it is not dated. For the patient, death has all the reality of an abstract noun.

The doctor sees death similarly as inevitable, but for him the time of death is not subjunctive. It relates to a specific cause: cardiac arrest, cancer, pneumonia, bullet wounds or a range of possible accidents. For the patient, life is basically a span of hopefully threescore and 10 years. For the doctor, life is subject to all the ills that "flesh is heir to" and can happen any time. Death for him is not an abstract noun but the result of a condition when a person, in medical terms, ceases to breathe.

Whether you incline toward the patient's or the doctor's view of life and death, the most depressing apparent conclusion is that human beings are all "sentenced to an end of life" from unnamed causes as a result of their having been born. This can leave people searching for life's meaning in spiritual terms or simply resigned to the inevitable. Underlying both is the ongoing struggle to survive, which is the common challenge of existence.

The major religions to which people turn for insights into the human condition stress the consoling and transcendental values that belief provides—often associated with a life to come, which instills in the believer an orientation to an eternal present in his future, a heaven, a return or reunion with God the Creator.

In this essay, however, I'd like to explore two additional ways of life that are fulfilling in the present and rooted in choice. Like all human choices, they are made in time but also are capable of transcending it. Whether they are given further spiritual meanings or not by the choosers or by the readers of this essay is not my intent. If certain responses exceed my stated purpose, so be it.

The first choice is an expression of love through action or the imagination. I do not think it is presumptuous to say that each of us is capable of doing something well and of loving what we feel within ourselves when we are doing it. It could be singing (as it was with Luciano Pavarotti or is with my granddaughter Anna) or running (as it was with Wilma Rudolph) or dancing (as it was with Fred Astaire) or working with wood (as it was and is with a man I will describe shortly) or anything that awaits being done well. No matter what it is, it absorbs and satisfies us completely. We just love to do it, and we love it most when we are doing it well.

I have a friend who recently retired as a university official. During his entire tenure at the university, he enjoyed himself most when he found time to work in his woodshop in the basement of his home. He made not only useful things like chairs and bookcases but works of art as well. Just a few days after his retirement, he and his wife converted the living room of their home into his workshop. Previously, he could only create what he called "wood art" in his spare time. Now he could do it whenever he chose and for as long as he chose. It was (and remains) his primary love and interest. It was and is an activity that fulfills him totally in the creative dimension of his life. Time is irrelevant.

Similarly, a nurse just recently retired and purchased a stone home a few lots north of my own. Spending much of her retirement pay, plus some of her life savings, on a decades-old house when she could have traveled or chosen a time-sharing residence in a warm climate is not common. I learned only recently that she lives alone but has two grown daughters. But it appears that to Alice—I know her only by her first name—restoring a home to its original quality and beyond could be (and every day is) a dream of continual progress.

First, she had the stones cleaned and edged where needed to restore their original color and shape. She replaced the windows and window frames as well as the garage door. She reshingled the roof. She hired a landscaper to create a new lawn along with new flower beds. She had the driveway repaved. In essence, she recreated the exterior front lot of the house, including the front porch. Then she restored an incipient swimming pool in the backyard, which she filled with filtered salt water. When I passed the house one day while she was standing in the driveway and told her how beautiful the restoration was, she said with a smile, "Wait 'til you see the inside."

Alice gave me the impression that what she was doing and had done was a truly crucial and pivotal period in her life. She seemed to be possessed by the same spirit that would possess artists or authors or dancers in the performance of the art they lived to create. Whether she would admit it or not, Alice was literally creating her own work of art. Like all artists, she was infusing her life into a projection of her tastes and choices in a house that would reveal her mark on it and would define it as hers, just as sculptures identify their sculptors, symphonies their composers, novels and poems their authors and plays their playwrights.

Whether it involves restoring a house or creating a painting, as Van Gogh did with the unique landscapes and inhabitants of the South of France, all artists put into their creations something of themselves, and they are the richer for it. And while they live, they live more bountifully. In a sense, they thumb their noses at death as an abstract noun or as a complete cessation of breath simply by choosing what they love to do and doing it. There may be obstacles, but obstacles have always been present where love is concerned. By choosing and doing what they love to do, the choosers prevail.

The second of the two choices for personal fulfillment is to make a life with one you love. Obstacles could exist here as well—family, age, ethnic or racial difference, as well as social status. The plight of Romeo and Juliet comes immediately to mind, along with its tragic consequences. It is one of the proofs of love that it challenges risk, as Romeo and Juliet realized, and their fidelity to that love is what immortalizes them. But it is one of the central truths of personal love that choice is often accompanied with mystery. Whether the one loved is someone met by chance or related, like a parent, brother or sister, is not decisive—at least not initially. But even when the relationship becomes undeniable and necessary, it can remain largely unexplainable.

Often when the happily married are asked what attracted or motivated them to choose one another, they find it difficult to put it into words. In the deepest sense, it cannot be put into words, which in itself is a testament to the truth that love does not lend itself to words—not completely. This is undeniably true with the happily married who may have been drawn to one another by attraction but whose voluntary union was based on choice.

How can a parent be drawn to one child more than to another—not in a spirit of competition or favoritism but in ways that do not lend themselves to explanation? The same may also be true for those who are totally unrelated. For example, from infancy to manhood, our son's love for his godmother never lessened. Sixty years between them made no difference. They could sit in the same room together, say little or nothing at all and be perfectly happy. Once she even let him cut her hair. Their relationship was a love like no other. That same attraction may exist between a man and a woman and be profoundly true but inexplicable.

When a chosen but otherwise mysterious love is conjugal, it confirms a union where each one is indispensable to the other. Each sees in the other someone to care for, as well as someone who cares. It proves among other things that love in the deepest and dearest sense is rooted in need—the need of each for each. Such a love, which is mutual, leaves the lovers themselves grateful but unable to determine—let alone explain—what draws them irresistibly to one another. Perhaps the ultimate proof of their love would be that each would be lost, distraught and incomplete if or when separated by distance or death. In fact, such separations only would intensify it.

What is indisputable about a true and chosen love is that the lovers find their mutual completion only with and in one another. Time for them is synonymous with presence when life reveals itself in all its fullness to each of them.

The fulfillment of love in union creates a completion between the lovers that resembles in many ways how pursuing fulfillment through action completes those who do what they love to do. The individuals in both instances refuse to be time's prisoners, while those who ignore the challenge and responsibility of love remain in servitude to what they need or want to survive. Whether they survive in penury, sufficiency or opulence, they remain the slaves of time.

The primary benefit that rewards those whose choices are motivated by love is that it redeems the choosers while they live. Life is no longer deemed worthwhile only by belief in some future reward or confirmation. It is completed in the act of loving that resulted from the choice, and the fulfillment stays within the chooser.

SAMUEL HAZO

The author of over fifty books of poetry, fiction, essays and plays, Samuel Hazo is the founder of the International Poetry Forum in Pittsburgh, Pennsylvania. He is also McAnulty Distinguished Professor of English Emeritus at Duquesne University, where he taught for forty-three years. From 1950 until 1957 he served in the United States Marine Corps (Regular and Reserve), completing his tour as a captain. He earned his Bachelor of Arts degree magna cum laude from the University of Notre Dame, a Master of Arts degree from Duquesne University and his doctorate from the University of Pittsburgh. Some of his previous works are *Becoming Done, The Less Said, The Truer, The Next Time We Saw Paris* (Poetry), *If Nobody Calls, I'm Not Home* (Fiction), *Tell It to the Marines* (Drama), *The Stroke of a Pen, Outspokenly Yours* and *Entries from the Interior* (Essays), *Snithereened Apart* (Critique of the poetry of Hart Crane), *The Pittsburgh That Stays Within You* (Memoir awarded the 2018 IPPY national bronze citation for creative non-fiction) and *The World Within the Word: Maritain and the Poet* (Critique). His translations include Denis de Rougemont's *The Growl of Deeper Waters,* Nadia Tueni's *Lebanon: Twenty Poems for One Love and* Adonis' *The Pages of Day and Night.* In 2003 a selective collection of his poems, *Just Once*, received the Maurice English Poetry Award. He has been awarded twelve honorary doctorates. He was honored with the Griffin Award for Creative Writing from the University of Notre Dame, his alma mater, and was chosen to receive his tenth honorary doctorate from the university in 2008. A National Book Award finalist, he was named Pennsylvania's first State Poet by Governor Robert Casey in 1993, and, while refusing a salary, he served until 2003.

www.ingramcontent.com/pod-product-compliance
Lightning Source LLC
LaVergne TN
LVHW051003080826
845145LV00009B/2436

* 9 7 8 1 7 3 5 4 4 0 4 9 1 *